new *life* within

a collaborative effort by Jillian Amodio

Crowdpublished for impact at CausePub.com

This book helps to provide care and encouragement to expectant mothers via pro-life organizations.

CausePub LLC
P.O. Box 63914
Colorado Springs, CO 80926

First ebook edition: 2013
First print book edition: December 2013

The publisher is not responsible for websites (or their content) mentioned in this book that are not owned by the publisher.

To learn more about CausePub and how to get involved in the next book project, visit CausePub.com or Twitter.com/CausePub.

ISBN: 978-0-9898139-2-1

Foreword

Brent L. Heathcott, Former Executive Director of Gabriel Network

I learned a long time ago that the best way to teach or communicate effectively – whether to an individual or a large group of people – is to tell a story. A good story. People are not only intrigued when they hear a good story, but they relate better to messages when they can frame them with people or events that they can understand, identify with or appreciate.

The stories of the women within these pages are more than just attention-getters – they are heroic. That is because in each instance, and whatever the circumstance, they chose life over death, goodness over evil, hope over fear. They heard and responded to the voice of God, encouraging them to be steadfast in faith. They have embraced motherhood and have seen the fruits of their love and labor over the years as they have watched their children grow.

Just like the women within the pages of New Life Within, I, too have a story to share, although not nearly as heroic! My story has two parts – journeys on which I am still travelling.

The first and most important journey was getting to know God and accepting Jesus Christ as my Lord and Savior. I was 30 years old when I intentionally made the decision to make Jesus the Lord of my life. At the age of 31, on Holy Saturday, 1998, I was baptized, confirmed and received first communion at Sacred Heart Catholic Church in Lombard, IL.

A lot of "life" happened to me and led me to that fateful evening in 1998. I was not raised in a religious home, and most of my decisions as a teenager and young adult reflected that reality. I was not what you would consider a classic "bad boy," but I definitely lived a typical secular life in high school and college. Ironically, both of my parents attended church when they were young and my father was actually in the seminary in the 1960s studying to become a priest in the Catholic Church, but both fell away from their faith in their 20s. While I would say my mother and father were good parents, we definitely did not have a Christian faith as the underpinning of our lives, actions and activities when I was growing up. However, my paternal grandmother was what most people commonly refer to as a "cradle Catholic," meaning she was baptized as a child and faithfully attended Mass her entire life. Up to and including the last days of her life before dying in 2011 at the age of 92, she attended daily Mass. In fact, the last time I saw my grandmother, she was settling into a pew for 5 p.m. Mass on a Saturday evening. She lived in Indiana and we were preparing to drive back home to Maryland. I held her face in my hands and said, "Goodbye, I love you." Since she had begun to experience the early stages of dementia, I figured it may be the last time I would see her alive. I was right – she died less than a year later.

When I was a child, my grandmother would invite me to church. Being happy to be invited anywhere by anyone, I always accepted. There is an important lesson for all of us in this – invite others to church, especially those who may be questioning their faith. Many times, people are curious and want to seek God for their lives, but they are just waiting for someone to invite them.

When I gave the homily at my grandmother's funeral Mass, I recalled those times and experiences and rightly credited her with giving me a faith foundation at an early age of which I was unaware, but that would serve me well in later years when I was searching for meaning in my life.

I think more than anything, having faith taught me to love. It led me to marrying my wife and, being blessed by God with our five healthy children.

As much as I love them, I think a relationship with Jesus Christ taught me even more to learn to love myself. Forgiveness is one of the best gifts we can give to another person in this lifetime, but sometimes the person we have to forgive most is ourselves. To this day, I still am working on loving myself as God loves me.

As much as I tried to fight it, the Holy Spirit was calling me almost immediately after my baptism to a greater commitment in serving Him and sharing the Gospel message. Although I fought it for years, I finally answered the call to enter the diaconate formation program in the Archdiocese of Baltimore in 2007. It was one of the most challenging and rewarding experiences of my life. It was hard – it pushed me outside of my comfort zone, which of course is exactly what God wanted for my life. My wife, Jill, and I had three children during my four years of formation and on a few occasions, I wondered if I had misinterpreted God's will and that perhaps he was telling me I needed to focus on my vocation as husband and father! I thought about quitting formation on a few occasions, but it was the Holy Spirit, through the wisdom of my wife, that convinced me to stick with it. Of course, they were both right.

On May 14, 2011, I joined 13 other men as we walked across the altar at the Cathedral of Mary Our Queen one at a time to put our hands in the hands of Archbishop (now Cardinal) Edwin O'Brien as he presented us with the Book of the Gospels and said, "Believe what you read, teach what you believe, practice what you teach."

And with that, I was a deacon in the Catholic Church, serving God's people in the Archdiocese of Baltimore.

This leads to the second part of my story and my other journey –serving His greater glory by using the talents, skills and professional experience I had gained over more than 20 years of my professional life.

Before joining Gabriel Network – an ecumenical Christian charitable organization in the state of Maryland serving women who are in poverty and/or facing homelessness while experiencing a crisis pregnancy – as executive director in 2013, I had worked for nearly 20 years in non-profit organizations, primarily health-care membership associations. During this time, I considered myself blessed and fortunate to work for mission-driven organizations whose primary purposes were improving human health. I worked with pediatricians, dentists, urologists, veterinarians and physician assistants – all in associations where I helped promote their missions through membership, leadership and program development. I learned valuable skills that served me well and ultimately, would lead me to serving a pro-life mission like Gabriel Network.

I had prayed to God for several years that if it was His will, to please put me in a situation where I could work in a Christian organization that served the less fortunate. Then one day, a friend of mine who knew of my heart's desire, emailed me a job opening at Gabriel Network and wrote, "I think this may be something you would be interested in…"

I joined Gabriel Network and that is where I met Jillian Amodio and so many wonderful people just like her who – everyday – fight the good fight against the secular world and against the pro-abortion forces that tell women who have been dealt a bad hand in life and find themselves pregnant that their only real option is to have an abortion.

It has been really amazing for me to witness how, if given a chance, many of the women we serve can flourish if just given an opportunity to have their child in a safe, nurturing and Christian environment. Many times, the women we serve suffer from mental and/or physical abuse, as well as physical or mental health issues. Almost all of them are in poverty. In almost every circumstance, the father of the baby is not in the picture. The women are alone and afraid.

Once they have made the crucial decision to choose life for their babies, they often wonder, "Now what? How will we make it?" That is where Gabriel Network has come into the equation for these women. In a nurturing Christian environment, we provide the stability and structure our client moms need in our three maternity homes to deliver their babies safely. At the same time, the women are preparing for the next steps in their lives as they move toward self-sufficiency. We also help hundreds of women a year in local communities where churches – Protestant and Catholic alike – establish Gabriel ministries of volunteers who journey alongside women who have not only practical needs, but emotional and spiritual needs as well.

It was the Archangel Gabriel who came to Mary to tell her she was to bear and give birth to Jesus, the Son of God, saying, "Do not be afraid…for nothing will be impossible for God." This is the basis of our ministry at Gabriel Network and the message of hope and faith that all of us in the pro-life movement must continue to embrace and cling to as we continue to serve women who are in great need because of a crisis or unplanned pregnancy.

I have been blessed to serve God in ministry and vocation – both as a deacon and professionally – in helping women make, and then embrace, the decision of choosing life. We have never looked into the eyes of another human being who is not loved by God, so Jesus calls us to show that love and mercy for the "least among us," meaning those who are in most need of our charity. It has been an honor working alongside Jillian, who has served Gabriel Network nobly, and so many other individuals who give so much of themselves to the pro-life cause and most especially, to women who find themselves in situations where it may be easy to choose against life, but have the courage, strength and faith to say "Yes" to life, just as Mother of our Lord did when the angel Gabriel appeared to her.

I hope you will enjoy and be inspired by the stories of the women within the pages of New Life Within. May God continue to bless you, your families and all brave women who continue to choose life – for themselves and their babies.

Acknowledgements

This book would not have been possible without the hard work, dedication, and willingness to share from all those involved in bringing this idea to fruition. Special thanks to our editor Amie McCracken, and to our team of proofreaders. I am eternally grateful for each of the women who were willing to share their deeply personal stories and for those who shared a funny kid moment. Thanks to Gail Centeno for the cover design. And of course thank you to the CausePub team for helping make this project a success.

Our hope is that this book will serve as a source of inspiration to all mothers regardless of what stage of life they may be in or what circumstances they may be dealing with. No matter who you are or what struggles you may be facing, you are not alone. A portion of the proceeds will go to support pro-life causes providing support to women facing crisis pregnancies and empowering them to choose life.

Table of Contents

"How can there be too many children? That is like saying there are too many flowers."

— Mother Teresa —

Unprepared for the Love
Ann Van De Water

The love starts the moment you feel the flutter in your womb—the first indication that life has blossomed there. No, I take that back; the love starts when you find out that there is new life blooming within you. Sometimes it shows itself as fear or anxiety about how things will go and how you will manage, but you will! Hopefully there will be days when you hug your belly and imagine finally meeting the little person growing there. The anticipation builds and builds over the months of pregnancy until you can hardly stand it! The hole in your heart can only be filled by that tiny being...God has planned it that way, and He never makes mistakes.

Then suddenly, they are here—in your arms, red, wrinkled, and probably screaming their head off.

I don't think I was prepared for the intensity of the emotions I felt for my babies as well as the passion I felt from their love for me. It is an amazing thing how God puts that fierce connection into both mother and child to create a bond that is sometimes overwhelming and at the same time intentionally indestructible. As a mom, I can't even imagine not loving my boys. I can't conceive of anything that they could ever do which would destroy that love. I may not always agree with their choices, their lifestyle, their words or actions, but they will always be my sons. I used to tell them when they were little: "I love you so much and even more, forever and ever, no matter what!" And it's true.

You fall head over heels instantly. You marvel at the incredible size of their minuscule fingernails and their shriveled tiny feet. You count every finger and toe and admire the rosebud mouth pursed and eager to suckle. You inhale and can't get enough of the new baby smell that permeates the room and fills your nostrils. You wish you could bottle that smell! These little precious gifts are at once helpless and demanding in their total dependence on you and you immediately and completely give yourself up to your mothering role. There is nothing you wouldn't do for this complete stranger who you know intimately. He has danced in your dreams and lived inside your heart for months now and you have been his source of life and strength!

I've always enjoyed talking to younger women about childbearing. Truth be known, I was none the wiser in the ways of obstetrics and all that meant before I was in the family way. You don't get it, unless you've been through it. Talk to any mom who braved the recommended nine, plus or minus, months of pregnancy and inevitably she has her own tale to tell about her experience. Some are humorous, some are truly horrifying (the deliveries in taxis, bathrooms, and elevators) and some are plain boring. It never ceases to amaze me when I hear of women in days gone by, giving birth in some field, wrapping up the new arrival and continuing with their labors (no pun intended!). Each tale is different, yet similar. We are all meant to have a gestation period of about nine months. Many of us train to deliver naturally; some of us strain to deliver naturally yet never get the chance to do so. Some go through countless hours of labor, which to us feel like days, only to end up in a C-section (yours truly)! Others waltz in as if it's another stop in their busy day and push that little sucker out like nobody's business in less time than it takes to bake a cake! I resent those women.

So, now you're a mom! How many of us started on this parenting adventure with the unrealistic, unattainable dream, declaring (if only to ourselves) that we wanted to be the "perfect" mom? I know I did. Guess what? I wasn't. If you're waiting to have children until you have your act together, you might as well forget it. If you're waiting to have kids until you can afford them, then you may well be past the child-bearing years before you are financially stable. If you're waiting to have them until you've read all the best books and you know you'll get it all right—here's a news flash! Having children is a labor of love with no instruction manual and every child is God's unique creation.

Yes, I wanted to be the perfect mom. Doesn't every mother? Our intentions are always wonderful! But life has a way of challenging all of us, even on our best days. They say experience is what you get when you don't get what you came for! It wouldn't have started with something called labor if it was going to be easy, and every mom's sentence is eighteen plus years of hard labor. Moreover, if we do our jobs right, they'll break our hearts and fly from our nests. If we don't do our jobs right, they'll break our hearts, come back to the nest, and live at home with us indefinitely. Seriously, if we play our cards right, we'll reap years of incredible relationships right on down through the generations. What a gift!

So, is motherhood the best thing ever, or do you feel like it's the hardest thing you have ever done in your life? Time moves on...they grow! Are you enjoying those special moments and noticing the time flying by or do your days drag, in an endless challenge of diaper changes, feedings, more diaper changes, and even more feedings? Do you feel alone on the path of motherhood? Do you believe you are the only one experiencing what you do in your daily grind? Are you floundering with sleep deprivation? Do you have the energy to even get dressed in the morning?

Here's the bad news: If you are a mom in the infant stage of child-rearing, it will be a while before the fog lifts. It will take two years before you can climb out of the servant phase of mothering. Your world needs to revolve around your child in the daily provision of shelter, food, clothing, and protection. There won't be many opportunities for vacations, girls' nights out, or luxurious long soaks in the tub. The only reading you will have time for are Mommy Blogs or pediatrician newsletters, and you will crave moments alone.

The good news is: You will never get enough of those amazing tiny fingernails and perfect pudgy feet. You will bathe them and marvel at the slippery miracle in your arms and fall in love every time. Before you know it, they will be mobile and you'll be into stage two.

If you are in the toddler stage, you have learned to don your running shoes early in the day, because that's all you'll be doing for a while. The bad news is: They have more energy than you and will get into everything! There's not much that isn't interesting and the world is theirs to explore and conquer! No matter what shape you are in, you'll always be struggling to stay a step ahead of the little rascals. They will learn the word "NO!" discipline will be tougher, and being clear, concise, and consistent will be critical!

Then in the blink of an eye, they'll be off to school and you will more than likely shed tears on their first day. You can't believe it—they seem so grown up all of a sudden.

You can shape them, teach them, and be a role model for so many important things in their lives. Their brains are taking in so much, and as Proverbs 22:6 says: "(if you) train them up in the way that they should go, when they are old, they will not depart from it." You can look for those teachable moments and instill in them the manners that matter and the character that will define them as they mature. Lead them now, mentor them when they are teens, and you will reap the harvest of a precious friendship when they are adults.

In no time flat, they hit high school, and you realize that in four years, they will be gone—off to college or pursuing their own dreams, fledged from the nest you have provided all these years. You unconsciously hold on tighter as they stretch their wings and seek their independence...and there is the rub! However, if you have done your job right, you will never lose them.

Therein lies the gift of generations of treasured relationships. If you lacked mothering in your life, or strong parenting models, know that you have the strength within and the resources at your fingertips to break those generational chains and be a great mom! Do it!

I know you all know this in your hearts, but I want to remind you again! The time flies by so fast. You will look back when you are mostly out of the storm and wonder how many blessings you missed in the frenzy of everyday life as a mom. You will question whether the things that seemed like a big deal really mattered after all; an unmopped floor, a failing grade, or a missed practice. You will long for the days when the toys were strewn all over the floor and the beds were left unmade, when you had to dig under piles of clothes and papers to find a missing sneaker that your teenager needed for an after-school soccer game. You will chuckle when you remember how they missed the bus and forgot their lunches more often than not.

Your tears will fall in the deafening silence.

These days the fridge stays fuller longer. The piles of laundry are small mounds compared to the overwhelming mountains they used to be, the shopping lists are shorter, and the days are longer. You will look back and wonder how you made it through. You won't be able to remember the blowups and the miscommunications, or the reasons for slammed doors. The little details of the trials and challenges you faced as they were growing up will become hazy and start to lose their significance. After all, most of our children will not become professional athletes, movie stars, Broadway divas, prima ballerinas, neurosurgeons, or virtuoso musicians. If they do, great! What you really want is for them to be happy with the paths they've chosen and the lives they are living. Now you can relax and gain a new perspective.

You thank God that your children are becoming their own people. You see glimpses more often of who God intended them to be and how He is molding them day by day. You want only the best for your children and what is really important is their character: their morals and values, their honesty and integrity, how responsible and respectful they are, how much they can fend for themselves once they have launched from your nest, and how much they are willing and able to contribute to society. You realize that there has been an indiscernible shift in the way you pray for your children. Suddenly it is easier to have this new perspective. You can see the forest through the trees.

It's the big picture that matters now. They are happy, well-adjusted, confident adults who love God and have purpose, direction, and love in their lives. Yes, deep unconditional love. If you can be at peace with having given them roots and wings, you can face the next season with joy!

What more can you ask for as a mom? Keep a sense of humor, seek God's face daily as you raise your little ones for Him, and enjoy the journey and the blessings He has given you.

Shifting Our Attachments
Dr. Barbara Sorrels

I believe the study of human development is a glimpse into the mind of God.

I love digging deep into scientific research as it relates to human development. Reading about the intricacies of brain development and the biological and psychological unfolding of human life is as much of a worshipful experience for me as sitting in church.

Recently I came across some fascinating information about the "maternal gleam." Babies are intensely interested in their mother's face and are intrinsically drawn to gaze at their eyes.

The intense gaze of the baby elicits a maternal gleam in the eyes of the mother, which locks mom and baby into an intense interaction where they seemingly drink one another in. The pupils of the mother's eyes dilate causing a reciprocal reaction in the eyes of the child.

The baby feels herself being felt by mom, and as this interaction takes place over and over, mom and baby fall in love—and form a secure attachment. The baby sees herself through the eyes of her mother and comes to know and believe that she is precious, and worthy of love and care.

One of the joys of my life is watching my daughter be a mom. Since they live in another city, much of my watching is done through video clips and photographs, but I have looked for, and seen, the maternal gleam. In our all-too-short visits, I see them drinking one another in. Little Eleanor is learning that she is the apple of her mom's eye and is feeling how her mom feels about her.

As I watch this dance take place between my daughter and granddaughter, it has caused me to be more mindful of the gleam in my Heavenly Father's eye. I'm still on that journey of growing and continuing to embrace His love for me. So often, my own history clouds my vision and I imagine His disappointment, anger and judgment. I am slowly learning to see myself in my Father's eyes and embrace His delight. You're a child too, His child.

For parents who are on the journey of making sense of your own story, gazing into the Father's eyes, and feeling the depths of His love, is one of the most healing experiences of all.

Take time to see yourself in your Heavenly Father's eyes.

"For you formed my inward parts; you knitted me together in my mother's womb. I praise you, for I am fearfully and wonderfully made. Wonderful are your works; my soul knows it very well. My frame was not hidden from you, when I was being made in secret, intricately woven in the depths of the Earth. Your eyes saw my unformed substance; in your book were written, every one of them, the days that were formed for me, when as yet there was none of them."

— Psalm 139:13-16 —

My Boys
Jessica Dugan

Motherhood is a dream that many women share. Like most females I know, I had dreamed of becoming a mother for as long as I could remember. I recall thinking of names that I would call my beloved children and daydreaming about what these precious little lives would look like.

While I often envisioned motherhood, my actual experience with becoming a mother was vastly different than the one my dreams had created for me. I have come to realize that there are some things in life that we simply cannot plan for and it is best to take each blessing as it comes.

At twenty years of age, I started dating the man who would later become my husband. Our relationship was going great. We had something special and I could see us building a future together. Little did I know, I was about to get the shock of my life. I suddenly found myself confronted with the surprising news that my boyfriend was expecting a baby with a previous girlfriend. I was not quite sure what to feel or how to react. At first I felt the dreams I had for us were shattered at my feet. I felt like I would never be able to have the picture perfect family of my dreams. I was faced with the seemingly impossible task of picking up these shattered pieces and deciding whether to throw them away or try to make something beautiful out of this unexpected situation. I was fearful that he and I would never be able to experience the joy of a first child together as a couple.

After much thought, I decided that the love we shared was strong enough to withstand any obstacles that this might bring. I made the decision to stand by his side and support him through whatever life brought our way. I knew deep in my heart that it would not be fair to abandon him at the time in his life when he most needed me and my support. Growing up in a similar situation, I had a unique perspective on how loving and influential a relationship with a step-parent can be. My step-father was a very active parent in my life.

When Colin was born, my life changed in ways that I could not have imagined. Our bond was instantaneous. He was so easy to love. He took to me well and the bond between us only continued to grow. I enjoyed every moment that I spent with him and knew that I could not possibly love him any more even if he were my own. I loved him with all my heart. When Colin was two years old, Sean and I decided that we were ready to give him a sibling. Sean was traveling and preparing for a deployment to Iraq. It was a stressful and tense time, but we knew that there was no better time to start expanding our family. On a short weekend visit, we decided that we would start trying for a baby. Before I was even late for a period I took a pregnancy test, I could not wait to find out if we were expecting. I was shocked and elated to find out that we were! I told Sean right around Valentine's Day that we would be bringing a new baby into our lives. Everyone was so excited for us. I had a difficult time working throughout my pregnancy. I was so sick and it seemed like a very long ten months. It was all worth the wait and discomfort when our sweet Paxton was born on October 10th.

Sean was deployed for the birth of our son, but I had the support and help that I needed from my friends and my family. The first time that our eyes met was a moment that simply cannot be described. He was, and will always be, perfect to me. Both of the boys are. I realized that although one child was physically a part of me, I truly loved each of my boys with the same intensity. Our bonds are unique and both boys are different. There is absolutely no greater love than the love between parent and child.

The boys are now three and six. Every day they learn something new and not a day goes by that they do not make me laugh or bring a smile to my face. Motherhood has taught me more than any other life experience. I thought I knew how motherhood would feel. I thought I knew what it would feel like to love my children and create a family. I realize now that I knew nothing. Until you experience it, until you actually become a mother, there is no way to fully comprehend the amount of love or the sense of wholeness you experience when you look into the eyes of your children. I have so much pride in both of the boys. They gave my life meaning and brought to light my true purpose in life. They give me strength and they give me hope. I continuously strive to be better and do better because they deserve nothing but the best.

I thank God every day for the life He has given me. I am so blessed to have been given the opportunity to raise both of my boys and to be given the chance to be the kind of mom that they can look up to. It doesn't matter how motherhood is bestowed upon you, it is the most precious and perfect gift that you will ever receive.

Something Beautiful

L. Rodgers
co-written by Jillian Amodio

I'm not even sure where to begin, but I will try my best to explain to you my road to motherhood. The story of my journey as a mother doesn't really begin with me, but started before I was even born. My journey to motherhood is rooted in the past. My family history isn't exactly the brightest of stories. There is heartache, lots of heartache. My father was born as the product of rape. Consequently, he was raised by his aunt and uncle. By the time my mom and dad met, my mother already had a son. My mother and father were married for several years and during the course of their marriage they had nine children together.

They belonged to a church, if it can even be called that. Really it can be more adequately described as a cult with the extremity of belief. Although we were a large family and maybe seemed happy on the outside, that couldn't have been further from the truth. My mom and dad were not happily married. My dad was abusive to both his wife and children, but my mother had been brainwashed into believing that she had to stay with him. When I was just a toddler, my parents finally decided to get divorced. I can't say that I remember very much about that time in my life, but I do know that my view of family and love was already skewed in the worst way. As I grew up I continued to suffer a certain amount of abuse and inevitable neglect as a result of being one of eleven children being raised by a single mother. There are many parts of my childhood that I don't remember, and the parts I can recall are far from being pleasant. As a teenager, I didn't understand the importance of purity or what it meant to love and be loved. I had no idea how love should be shown or what it felt like to be received.

The first time I was ever faced with the idea of having a child was when a close friend of mine tragically decided to have an abortion. In some odd way, I felt like it was my fault. I felt like maybe I didn't do a good enough job in persuading her not to have the abortion, or maybe I didn't give her enough love and support. Out of this guilt came a decision that I still can't fully understand.

My boyfriend at the time was also a close friend of the girl who had the abortion. Both of us felt responsible and were plagued with guilt. We felt an intense need to make things right. We felt that we ourselves needed to atone for the death of her baby. Together we decided to try and have a baby of our own to replace the innocent life that had been lost. We tried for six months and it never happened. Our relationship ended shortly after, leaving my heart completely shattered. I left my heart open, and he was my first serious relationship. I let myself fall in love, or at least fall into what I thought was love, only to be left brokenhearted and defeated.

Shortly after, a close friend of ours killed himself. I couldn't take any more loss. I cried and cried for weeks on end. I cried inconsolable tears of despair. I cried all day long; while I was driving, working, in class, even as I fell asleep. At first I think that I was crying for my broken heart. Then it turned into crying over the loss of my friend. Then I was caught in a downward spiral and I began to cry for everything. I was lost. I was hopeless; I was so deep in depression that I wondered if I could ever come out of it.

Finally, I literally let out a cry of complete surrender and hopelessness. I lifted that cry up to God and surrendered my life to Him. Alone I was dying, it was a slow painful death that began in my soul and I knew I needed to be saved. I threw myself into church and was going as often as I could. At church I faced my sins and my pain. I began to allow God to take away my pain and replace it with His healing grace.

I was still very confused. During the times I wasn't at church, I found other ways to numb my pain. I still partied, I drank, and I slept with people I didn't know. I refused to allow God to be a part of my life every day, only when I needed Him the most.

When it came time for me to go to college I applied to one place and got in. I started in the fall at a private Christian college. I'm not sure why this was the only place I applied to, but I guess God knew that it was where I needed to be. My first year there didn't go very well. By the end of the spring semester I had pretty much gotten myself kicked out and was not allowed to return in the fall. I spent another summer numbing myself from all of the pain and disappointment in my life. My cheerleading coach ended up contacting me a few weeks before school was scheduled to start in the fall. She had managed to pull some strings and worked it out so that I could return to school in the fall. Shortly after starting school again, I met a guy. I had no desire to date anyone, but I agreed to be his girlfriend anyway. About a month after we started dating, we found out that we were pregnant. I had gone into a gas station to take the test. I can't even remember what my first thoughts were when I saw that it was positive.

The first thing I can actually remember is getting back into the car with my boyfriend. I threw the test at him and said, "I hate you." We drove around in silence for nearly an hour. I suggested we take another test. I was hoping that maybe the first one had been wrong. I came out of yet another gas station bathroom with yet another positive pregnancy test. We sat in my car and looked at each other. "What are we going to do?" we both asked. We responded in the only way we knew how, by throwing our arms around each other and crying.

I could go into the details about how we had to decide that we were going to quit school and how he was going to join the Army. The only thing that really matters though is what came out of it. Through my pregnancy, I was finally able to see and feel everything that God had been doing in my life. I believe that God made this baby for me. I believe that God made this baby for his father. I believe that this baby was God's gracious gift, because I know we didn't deserve him.

What's even more insane is that God didn't stop there. He also created great passion between my boyfriend and me. I was seven months pregnant when I married my boyfriend and the father of my child. I can't even say that it was the baby that made me marry him, or that my husband and I are an amazing match, but through God's grace we were blessed with an amazing love. I've always felt like the choices that I have made in my life have gone completely against everything that I've ever thought I would do. If I was someone on the outside looking in at my life and all of the choices I have made, I would think that I was the stupidest person in the world. I can't try and explain every detail of how I felt and why we made the choices that we did, but I can say that through it all; from even before I was born, to where I am now, God has had everything in His hands. He has been in complete control of my hectic life. When my life and the people in it were completely out of control, God still had me in His hands.

I am living a beautiful life. We have two wonderful boys. Though I have many days where I am still dealing with depression, guilt, or shame from the life I have led, I still know that I am blessed. Sometimes I struggle with feeling like I'm not a good enough mom, but God is on my side. I have been extremely blessed by my children, and I am so blessed by a God who loves me. I adore my husband who has given me the opportunity to be a stay-at-home mother. Knowing how much I love my family gives me an idea of how much more God loves me. Knowing how many times God has shown me grace, I strive to do the same for my family. I am beginning to understand how my savior could have wanted to die for someone as lost and broken as me, because I know that I would give my life for the ones I love. My children are amazing, but the true miracle is that God has been able to take the struggle, the heartbreak, the death, and the pain, and He has been able to turn it into something beautiful.

"I love how toddlers interpret their world. My two-year-old son wears these jeans that always seem to be slipping off his barely-there-behind. One day I said to him, 'Caed, you're saggin' your wagon!' a phrase I'm sure I picked up from my mother. Later that day, he came to me and, looking concerned, said, 'Mommy! My wagon falling off!' It was. And usually is."

— Alyssa De Jong —

Dear Baby
Kristi Dalnoky

Dear Baby,

How could I have known how you were going to change my life?

I used to spend hours in front of a mirror; I'd brush my hair, my long, thick hair. I'd paint my nails and lotion my legs after a long, hot bath. I knew every freckle, every scratch, every detail of myself. After all, who else did I have to pay attention to each day and night? Then you came into my world, and I have traded those tendencies for a new form of pampering. You. I would trade all the beauty tools, manicures, bubble baths...anything to spend my time running tired fingers through your feather-soft curls; scrubbing your teeny toes as you splash me wildly with lukewarm bath water; massaging lavender-scented baby cream all over your sweet, soft skin. I have memorized every inch of your God-painted canvas. I know that you have a second piggy on that pudgy little foot that bends slightly to the left, and I could draw that round birthmark with my eyes closed. You are precious to me. Until I held you in my arms, I never fully understood how precious you would be to me.

I sang to you in the car every morning on the drive to work. Before I knew if you were a girl or boy, and you were a wriggling little bean in an ever-expanding bump, I'd sing. It was my time to be loud—to be quiet. I'd sing to you, for you, at you. Sometimes I would sing to you a praise song at the top of my voice, and other times, I'd whisper you a lullaby. How would I have ever known that those car ride serenades would seem so small in comparison to the songs to come? As I cradled your newborn body in my arms each night, singing over your tininess, I would melt inside at the awesome revelation that God says He sings over me too. Just as I sang over you, He sings over us. (Zephaniah 3:17) That alone would have been enough to make motherhood amazing, but then, you got a little bigger, and one night, you decided to sing my song right back to me. How could I have ever known that your voice would make such an imprint on my soul? That the soundtrack of my happiness would come from your lips?

Your innocence is the light in my world. Your laughter, my favorite sound. I thought I was creative, until I heard you playing make-believe and realized that your imagination is genius. You read my eyes and know me. You heard my heart beating from the inside, and somehow, I think you always will.

You call me Mommy. I call you tangible joy. You call me Mother. I call you Baby. You call me Mama. I call you Angel.

No one on Earth loves me like you do. No one on Earth needs me like you do. No one on Earth sees me like you do. I say Earth, because I know where your love for me comes from. It comes from the same heart that has gifted me with my love for you: God. I have loved you with an everlasting love. You love, because I first loved you. (Jeremiah 31:3 and 1 John 4:19)

Dear Baby, I don't know what life has in store for you and me, but if what has been is any indicator as to what is coming...it will be nothing short of heaven.

"When my sons were just seven and five years old, my mommy-sixth sense revved into high gear, as things had suddenly gotten very quiet upstairs. So I stealthily climbed the stairs to peek into their room and find out what they were up to with their neighbor buddy. They had all gotten down to just underwear and were taking turns at the windowsill to find out who had the best equipment and greatest capacity to hit the neighbor's house by peeing out the bedroom window! It is so hard to discipline when all you want to do is burst out in peals of laughter!"

– Ann Van De Water –

For These Reasons and More
Deanna Herrmann

When I found out I was pregnant, I cried. I walked up to my husband, with a lump in my throat, and pointed to the bathroom where the small plastic wand had just shown us that our lives were about to change forever. My husband says my face was as white as a ghost and he couldn't imagine what kind of terror awaited him in the bathroom. When he saw our fate lying on the counter, he smiled and hugged me, but I cried. He was happy; I was terrified.

From the time I was a young girl and through most of my adult life, I never wanted children. I have never been the kind of girl to ooh and ahh over the cute little babies you see while out shopping or walking in the park. I had a babysitting job, as did every teenage girl, but I did it for the money. I played with my Barbie as a child, but never really baby dolls. I never felt this maternal instinct or need nor did dreams of my future include children.

You see, when I was three years old, my mother gave birth to my brother who ended up being diagnosed with Trisomy II Distal Short Arm Chromosomal Disorder—a rare genetic defect. My father was an unknowing carrier of this defect that is severe in its nature. The doctors informed my parents that my brother would most likely not survive past six months old. My brother ended up living to be seventeen years old and survived what I consider to be a painful and cruel life. He had epilepsy; cerebral palsy; was blind, delayed, couldn't walk; had food allergies and intolerances; and was never able to speak, eat, or do anything on his own. In essence, he was a baby his whole life.

As a child, I was protective of him and I loved him. As I grew older, the love turned into resentment for both him and my mother. I was a selfish teenager craving a childhood. I felt robbed and cheated. I wanted to actually play on the volleyball team after being successful in try-outs. I wanted to join the dance squad. I wanted to stay in band. I wanted to have friends over and go to their houses. However, these things were not possible because my mom worked, as did my step-father, and I had to be home from school to care for my brother. My anger and resentment grew, as did the distance I placed between my family and myself.

I left home at seventeen in search of the freedom I felt so tremendously deprived of. I declared my life as my own. I was going to live it any way I wanted. I admitted to being selfish with my time. I told my mother to expect to not have grandchildren. I told the men I married to never expect children.

I made mistakes in my life because I didn't know myself. I suffered through abuse and violence. I turned to drugs and alcohol. For a long time, I was still a reckless and rebellious teenager. I had a deep desire, almost a need, to punish the world for what I felt I had lost. I also wanted to punish myself for who I was becoming. Somehow, though, I made it through. With the help of good friends and guardian angels I'm sure were meant to cross my path, I chose a different road than the one I was so clearly headed down. I chose to rise above and become a survivor. Sadly, my first marriage was one of the casualties of me finally accepting the past, letting it go, and becoming the woman I deserved to be.

Suddenly, it was 2009, I was finishing my graduate degree and on my second marriage which was failing. I had followed this military man all the way to Germany, given up my career, my friends, my family, and I was determined to make it work. I knew I married the wrong man, but I thought that by having a child I could save my marriage and myself. I was still on the fence as far as whether or not I really wanted a child. Both the idea of having one and not having one scared me. Still unsure of what I desired, we pathetically tried for a baby and did not get pregnant. By this time, I was thirty-two years old and was convinced that having a baby was also not in the cards. Things only grew worse between us and ultimately we divorced. I declared that my heart was forever closed. No more marriage. No more love. No more relationships.

On Christmas Eve I sat alone, still in my house in Germany, feeling sorry for myself. I was impatiently waiting on circumstances that would allow me to return home. I was beating myself up for another failure. I really just wanted to sit alone in the darkness and cry. However, a friend of mine had convinced me to come out and at least drown my sorrows with her at a bar. Sure, why not? She had also convinced another friend of hers in a similar situation to do the same.

When I saw him, it was the most unbelievable attraction I could ever imagine. All I knew is that I felt drawn to him. But I was set on being miserable and sat at the bar alone while my friends went out to dance. Then, he spoke to me and we struck up a conversation. It came so easily and it was fun. It felt so good that I just went with it. I told him right then and there about my current marital situation. He told me about his recent break-up. We discovered how much this German boy and American girl had in common. It was a great night, but I was in a dark place. I pushed him away for a while until I pushed so far I thought he was going to give up. That's when I realized just how much I was in love. I couldn't imagine life without him and despite the worst possible timing, this was happening and it was amazing.

I decided to indulge myself and accept his love and give him mine. He became my best friend. We had the whole package, friendship and passion. Unfortunately, I was leaving in a few months. We made the best of the seven months we had in Germany before I had to return to America. I was terrified of making another relationship mistake, but I knew this was different. If I had known that this is what love was supposed to be like, I would have never settled for anything less. I couldn't let him go, so I had to take the next step. We decided to fight to maintain our relationship over the 4,500-mile distance. I felt this would be a good test for us, to make sure we weren't just swept up in a moment. It would also give us both time to find ourselves again while still being together.

The distance did not weaken us, but made us stronger. One year later, his visa was approved and he gave up everything, moving to America to be with me. The requirements of his visa only gave us ninety days to get married, so we did it the first week he was home. Four short weeks later, we learned we were going to be a family of three, which brings this story back to where it began.

I was frightened to be pregnant. I was thirty-five, which is considered advanced maternal age for having a child, adding to the concerns surrounding this pregnancy considering my family history. I had this foreboding feeling; I convinced myself it would end up a disaster. I thought only the worst and prepared myself for all of the genetic testing possible. If I were to have a child with my brother's genetic disorder, I would abort. Notice the use of "I" in the past few sentences. This was not a decision I was consulting my husband about. I would not relive my childhood. And there it was, the reason for my fear, the reason for holding back all of these years. My husband and I have only really argued a couple of times throughout our entire relationship, and this was one of those times.

We went to our appointment and heard the baby's heartbeat for the first time. It was so powerful that I was shaking and crying, my husband just smiling. It was an experience I could never describe in words. It changed me. That moment overwhelmed me with love, maternal love. This little being was growing inside me, depending on me for life and safety. How could I have ever thought about ending it? How could I have ever thought about excluding my husband from that decision? How could I lose something so beautiful that was made with love and given as a blessing? Simply, I could not.

I decided to let go of the reigns and place my faith in God. I didn't have *any* of the genetic testing. I carried on with my pregnancy as normal and fell more in love with our baby every day. The fear was always in the background, but it was silenced with prayer as well as love from my husband.

Our son is happy, healthy, and soon to be eighteen months old. It hasn't been an easy road. The timing wasn't the best. We have had to make many sacrifices, and our lives have truly changed drastically. If I'm being honest, I do sometimes mourn the loss of the life I had before. I can't tell you that it's all sunshine and rainbows because being a parent is hard work and full of sacrifice. I can tell you whole-heartedly, however, that it is worth every second, every sacrifice, and every beautiful changing moment.

When I saw and held my son for the very first time, I felt changed forever; I knew I had become his mother.

When I saw my son complete a first, such as walking, I knew I had become his teacher.

When I held my son, who ran to me after falling down, I knew I had become his protector.

When I look at my son, I see pieces of myself. It's both inspiring and beautifully overwhelming.

When I see him smile, my heart becomes so full that my eyes fill with tears.

My son helps me see the world through a child's eyes, so in a sense, he has given me the one thing I thought I lost, my own childhood.

For these reasons and more, for all that our children help us to become, it is worth it.

Why We Repeated Our Daughter's First Nine Birthdays

Rachael Moshman

My husband and I adopted our daughter when she was nine years old. She was abused and neglected her first four years and then bounced around foster care for the next five.

Amazingly, she was still willing to trust us. She was still willing to give loving us a shot.

It was—and still is—hard work for all three of us, but she's attached. We're a family. We love each other. We're her parents, and she's our baby.

Birthdays are challenging for her. They remind her that she wasn't always ours and make her think of all of the hard times she had before us. She often tells us that she wishes we were her first parents, in addition to her last.

She's twelve now and in middle school. She doesn't want to grow up. She wants to be a little girl. She isn't seeking the same level of independence as her peers. She finally has a mommy and daddy who truly love her, take care of her, and keep her safe; she isn't ready for this chapter of her life to close. She missed out on too much.

One morning she was sobbing that she wished she was only six, and an idea popped into my head. We missed out on her first nine birthdays. Her tenth birthday was the one we were part of and it was the only birthday party she'd ever had.

I decided to redo all of the others.

We started with her first birthday. I decorated with free printables I found online. I gave her a birthday crown to wear. We sang "Happy Birthday" and ate mini cupcakes. We talked about the milestones children usually hit at that age and what her first birthday would have been like if she had been with us then. We played "Ring Around the Rosie." We even gave her gifts to unwrap! (They were possessions she already owned: a playground ball for her first birthday redo.)

We continued the celebrations over the next couple of weeks. Some of the celebrations were painful and filled with tears.

During her fifth birthday redo party, she shared that she was sad because she knew that must have been a really difficult birthday for her since it was the first one she spent in foster care.

Her ninth birthday redo was especially heavy because she was in the midst of a very traumatic situation that year.

I tell her all of the time that the only way to process the hard stuff is to deal with it. These birthday redo celebrations have helped her with that. She now has a file folder in her brain of good memories from these little family parties—plus dozens of photos! Hopefully the positive memories will outweigh the negative in time.

"When one of my sons was in middle school, I commented to him about how he was looking more and more like me as he got older. He said, 'I know, I am getting a mustache.'

..."

— Desiree Albo —

My Unexpected (Lovely) Life
Amanda Perry
co-written by Jillian Amodio

I was never one of those people who desperately wanted children. I never dreamed of having a huge family with a whole bunch of kids running around. I wanted a career in the military, I wanted to be me. When I was seventeen, a senior in high school, I got the shock of my life. I found out I was pregnant.

I remember the day I found out, I felt like the world was caving in. I was terrified. I had bought a pregnancy test and took it in the bathroom at Safeway. I was too afraid to take it at home for fear that my parents would find out. When I read the result and realized that it was positive, I started to cry. I called my cousin in tears. I was begging her to adopt my baby. Here I was, minutes after realizing that I was pregnant, and I was already trying to give my baby away. I was scared, I was confused, and I felt so alone.

The thought of abortion never crossed my mind. For me, that was not an option. I did this, I was going to have to deal with it, I just couldn't see myself raising a child at seventeen years old. As I cried to my cousin on the phone, I pleaded with her over and over again. "I cannot be a mom." I said. "Please, please adopt this baby." I had so many thoughts running through my mind.

As the shock wore off and the reality of the situation began to set in, I thought for sure that if my cousin took the baby it would be best for everyone. I would still be able to see the baby even though I was not ready to be a mom. My cousin is five years older than me, she already had a daughter and we have always been more like sisters than cousins anyway. This was the plan for a while. I knew it wasn't perfect, but I thought it was the best decision I could make.

When it came time to tell my parents, I was nervous and scared. I didn't know exactly how they would react, but I knew they would be upset. My parents were divorced, and I was living with my dad. My aunt told my mom for me, and my mom tried to convince me to have an abortion. My mom was scared for me. She had a baby when she was a teenager and she put it up for adoption. At that time I was sixteen weeks pregnant. I had already gotten used to the idea that there was a baby, a new life, growing inside of me. Abortion was never an option.

When I told my dad, he didn't get angry; he just told me that he was really disappointed. My step-mother actually grounded me for being pregnant. By this point I had grown used to the idea of being a mother. I no longer wanted to give my baby up to anyone even if it was my own cousin. I had made the decision to keep the child I was carrying, the child I had created. After it became clear to everyone that I had decided to keep the baby, I had to find a place to live. My dad wanted to help as much as he could but my step-mom insisted that she would not live in a house with a baby.

My baby's father didn't believe that it was his. He moved out of state while I was pregnant and wanted DNA confirmation that the baby was in fact his. After our daughter was born, he didn't even meet her until she was over a year old.

Throughout my pregnancy, my parents made sure that all of the responsibility was mine alone. It was my problem, and I had to deal with it. When I was six months pregnant, my mom finally came around and told me that I could live with her once the baby was born.

I worked hard throughout my pregnancy. I stayed in school as a full-time student and worked two jobs. I was determined not to give up on my dreams and goals. I had come to the conclusion that I could handle this. I was going to make a good life for myself and my baby. Friends were somewhat supportive, but it became clear that we now had very different priorities. Some friends kept telling me how exciting it was that I was going to have a baby. And it was exciting, but they also didn't realize how difficult it could be. Other friends made sure to continuously tell me that I was ruining my life. I was happy. I really was, but I also felt a lot of confusion.

Things started to get better once I graduated. At nine months pregnant, I walked across the stage and received my diploma. After my daughter was born, I went to college and got really good grades. At times it was really difficult, but I made it work.

When Ariel was born, all of the confusion, all of the fear, and all of the difficulty that I had experienced throughout my pregnancy faded away. None of it mattered anymore. I was holding this precious little girl in my arms and I had never felt so much love.

Although I was living with my mom, it was still hard at times. She had to work and I was basically a single mom. I loved my daughter so much, and I knew that I was strong enough to take care of both of us. Cuddling with my daughter, holding her close, seeing this precious life I had created made it all worthwhile.

I dated a few people and had a few failed relationships before I decided that I was going to focus on myself and my daughter. If I was meant to meet someone, then it would happen when it was supposed to. I had to focus on what was important at that moment. When my daughter was seventeen months old, I met Jason. He was really nice and incredibly supportive of the fact that I was a single mom. I was not looking for a relationship, but the more we talked the more I realized that he was someone special.

I didn't let Jason meet my daughter for a while, but once he did, he fell in love with her. After a few months it became clear to both of us that we were meant to be together. We moved in with Jason's parents after we were married. Shortly after, we found out we were expecting another baby! We started saving money right away so we could buy our own house.

This time, things were so different. We wanted this baby so badly and we were incredibly excited to be a family. Everyone was happy, there was no disappointment, no fear, just love and joy. We bought our first home together one month before our second child, Amelia, was born. It felt so good to finally be a family.

Ariel was always such an easy child, it was almost like she knew how difficult life was for me. She has truly been a blessing. She was almost three when Amelia was born and immediately took to her little sister with a tremendous amount of love, attention, and care. By the time she was four and a half, we had welcomed our third daughter, Alaina, into the family.

My children have taught me so much about life and love. Love will happen. It just happens when we least expect it. Looking back now it's funny. I used to think that kids were annoying; I never wanted any for myself. Shortly after finding out I was pregnant, it was like this switch flipped on, and all of a sudden all I could think about was babies. I am so in love with being a mom. The moment I held my baby in my arms, I could not fathom ever leaving her for extended periods of time. My children and my family are my life. It turns out that my worst fear has become my greatest joy. Having a child at eighteen is the best thing that has ever happened to me, she gave me life.

The life I am living is far different than the one I had planned. I never thought I would be a stay-at-home mom with three kids. Our family is so happy and our life is far better than any of us ever could have imagined.

For anyone who may be experiencing the same kind of situation I found myself in, I know it is scary and I know it is hard, but believe me it will all be okay. I did it and so can you. It may seem like the world is crashing down, like your life is ending, but trust me, your life is just beginning.

Motherhood:
The Deadliest Catch
Stephanie Messa

Outside of extreme crab fishing, being a mother is maybe the most terrifying station in all of Christendom. I remember when the doctor placed our oldest son on my chest for the first time. He was purplish and slimy and screaming and so very small. Not even taking into consideration the fact that Ladytown (aka the Baby Maker, aka the Cave of Wonders, aka the birth canal) had just been through obstetric torture, I was overcome with feelings. So many feelings. For starters, I wasn't even quite sure how to hold the thing, and I had held many babies before him. I was so afraid the gelatinous baby-slug was going to slide right out of my arms. He was angry and cold and confused, and I wondered how on Earth I was ever going to be able to keep this child happy and healthy into adulthood with all teeth present and accounted for.

The first weeks and months were rough but by no fault of Jude's because he was, by all accounts, a very easy baby. I was coming down off of a sweet lady cocktail of raging postpartum hormones and stabilizing regular hormones. And while I'd like to blame the ebb and flow of those wicked, wicked hormones, my psychosis lay simply in the lap of this revelation of motherhood. When he would cry, I wasn't always sure what he wanted. I would get this very crazy and stressed feeling inside that made my skin ache because it was my job to help him and I didn't know how to do it. I would lay awake at night thinking of all the terrible things that could happen to him and how I could possibly stop them. You see, I have what some would call an overactive imagination. I call it "an absurd and impossible worst-case scenario preparedness plan." I had escape routes mentally mapped out for each street in my neighborhood should a murderer van pull up beside us while out for a walk. At gas stations and parking lots, I kept my key clenched in my fist with blade facing out in the event that kidnappers came and needed a good shivving. I was a nutcase (I say "was" like I've somehow outgrown it—I wish).

As he grew, I realized the reason I was so stressed and afraid (and always on the lookout for predators and rabid dogs) was because he was my very own heart. My own heart was walking (or crawling and drooling) outside of my body and was completely susceptible to various kinds of evils and there was only a limited amount of protection I could offer. By becoming a mother, I had made myself more vulnerable than I could ever be outside of this position in life. I was fully exposed in the form of a very small and essentially helpless human and that is a scary reality.

Believe it or not, there's beauty to this reality too. My husband said it so well. Having a child is like having thousands of exposed nerve endings. When something hurts your child, be it physically or emotionally, it burns every part of your being. Likewise, when they experience joy and happiness, you're filled with more extreme gladness than you thought was possible. When Jude is happy, I'm thrilled. When he thinks something's funny, I think it's hilarious (except when what he thinks is funny is me telling him not to dive bomb the dogs from the kitchen table for the tenth time today). When Jude succeeds, I excel more than I ever could on my own. His success is my greatest joy not just as a mother but as a human on this Earth.

If I had never become a mother, I would still experience fear, sadness, joy, and success. Now, as a mother, I experience these emotions and more hundred-fold. I am as vulnerable as that newborn purple and gooey slug-baby that marked the beginning of this mothering adventure/nightmare. I am also as filled with love as the two-year-old tyrant that takes a break from "snocking" bad guys to say, "I love you, Princess Mommy." I have willingly opened myself up to extreme pain and pleasure all in one act and it makes me feel like I am really living. Like I'm experiencing the full vibrancy of life (and the full vibrancy of Crayola markers when applied to the walls of my home by tiny hands). As a mother, I will always experience fear but my heart will always be full.

"I once took my kids, plus my daycare kids, (nine kids total) to see the movie *Rugrats in Paris*. I parked my fifteen-passenger van and started to help unbuckle each child. My four-year-old son looked around the parking lot and suddenly started to cry. All of a sudden, he screamed 'We are not in Paris! You said we are going to see the Rugrats in Paris. We are not in Paris!'
He was mad until the movie started."

— Pam Squillari —

A Beautiful Mistake
Anna Schatzman

Being a mother is my calling. My daughter is my life, my world. And to think I almost ended her precious life...

As I looked in the mirror three years ago I looked at the reflection of a woman who today I barely know; an addict, self-centered, dependent. I touched my slightly rounded belly. I knew I was pregnant but I could not bring myself to believe it.

I ran out of the bathroom to tell my husband. He cracked a half smile and said, "Surprise?" I went back to the bedroom and laid down on the bed. Into my mind crept a nasty lie.

"God, why have you forsaken me?"

I know the night that we conceived very well. My husband lied to me. A lie that cut me to my soul. It was the biggest lie he had ever told, and I was sick just thinking about it. We were drinking, partying, and having a blast. His best friend was deploying to Afghanistan and he asked if we could split up and go our separate ways for the remainder of the night. I was hurt, but thought to myself, boys will be boys.

I asked where they were going and my husband told me they were just going up the street to a little bar. "We are just going to go shoot some pool," he said.

Later that night when we met back up at our apartment I asked if they had enjoyed themselves. I again asked where they went.

"Just a little bar, I can't remember the name," he replied.

I knew he was lying. I don't have many requests in our marriage. There was one request however, that I would not stand to be ignored.

No strip clubs.

I used to be one of those girls. I used to dance in a strip club. It was absolutely the last place in the world I would ever want my husband to be. He continued to lie until he finally admitted his betrayal. I was crushed. We had only been married for a few weeks and already I knew that we had made a mistake. He pushed for forgiveness and I remained trapped in my despair.

Finally, I gave in and I showed him forgiveness in what I thought was the best way I knew how—sex.

Passion and drunkenness are a lethal combination when you are not ready or prepared for the consequences that can follow unprotected sex. The next morning I woke up to go to work as a waitress. I lived day to day on whatever little cash I made during my shifts.

A few hours later I left with the $40 I had made that day. I found myself at the pharmacy counter talking with a pharmacist.

"I'd like to buy the Plan B pill," I said to the pharmacist.

"That will be $59.99."

"Oh," I said, clearly disheartened. "I can't afford that."

"I'm sorry, but it is not covered under insurance," she replied.

I left confused and afraid. *I guess I am going with Plan C*, I thought to myself.

A few days later I took a pregnancy test. Much to my relief it was negative. Life went on as usual. Drinking, partying, smoking… I had myself convinced that I was not pregnant but somewhere deep inside I knew the truth.

Eight weeks later is where I found myself staring in the mirror at a woman I hardly recognize anymore. The reflection of a person who was self-centered, reckless, addicted, broken, and hopeless.

I don't recognize that person anymore. Praise God. Here is a passage from my personal diary.

June 27, 2011

Dear Diary,

For the first time in my life I can understand God's infinite love for me. As I hold my daughter in my arms, as I stare into her innocent eyes, I thank God for His love for me. I have been sober for six months now, and I want to be the best mom that I can be. Thank you, God, for allowing me the gift of motherhood. She is my life. She is my Emma.

You will never understand fully the gift of the baby inside of you until you hold her in your arms. My life is forever changed. I am a proud wife to an amazing father. My husband is so loyal, faithful, hardworking, and loving. He has come a long way and so have I. Being a mom is my greatest joy in life. My days are filled with laughter, pearls, bows, and new opportunities to grow in love with my daughter daily. I am a disciple of Christ, friend, daughter, wife, mother, and recovering addict. Every day I make a choice to be better than I was the day before.

Maybe you know me because when you look at your reflection you see yourself as I was.

What started as a mistake became my greatest blessing. I think back on the day I held $40 in my hand, ready to choose my own path. Had it not been for His divine intervention, I could have robbed myself of motherhood, and my child of life.

"Of all the rights of women, the greatest is to be a mother."

— Lin Yutang, Chinese writer —

Pure Love
Jillian Amodio

As a child I had this baby doll who went everywhere with me. Her name was baby Jennifer. Baby Jennifer was my most prized possession; although I am not quite sure that possession is the right word, for I loved her as if she were real. I bathed her, I read to her, I sang to her, I slept with her. She came on family vacations, rode in a baby stroller, and knew my every secret. Baby Jennifer was as real to me as any other baby.

Baby Jennifer was a Christmas gift one year and from the minute I opened the box and lifted the delicate baby doll out of it, I had never seen such a beautiful baby.

When my uncle would playfully toss her around I would cry out for him to be gentle with her. When she would no longer hold water (she was a water baby) without leaking, my grandmother and I took her to the doll hospital. I waited anxiously while the kind woman with gentle eyes and soft weathered hands cradled my baby and tried to think of what to do. This doll hospital catered mainly to porcelain and antique dolls, and the woman sadly handed my baby back to me and said, "I'm sorry dear; there is not anything we can do to fix a water baby." She suggested that we contact the manufacturer.

My seven-year-old heart was broken. I was not shipping my baby back to some factory to be disposed of. She was mine and I was going to care for her, broken or not.

My grandmother knew just what to do. She had a plan. My grandmother and I, we have a special bond. There is no woman quite like my Nani. She knew just what this doll meant to me, and she made an unexpected stop at the craft store on our way home.

I looked at her quizzically and questioned what we were doing there. Couldn't she see I was grieving? This was no time for crafts. She led me down the aisles until she found what she was looking for—a bag of plastic beads, the kind that some stuffed animals are filled with. "This should do," she said.

My heart lifted and I realized that my Nani had once again come to my aid. When we arrived home, my Nani did some minor surgery on baby Jennifer. She cut open the valve on the back of my baby, the one that was supposed to keep water from leaking. She grabbed a funnel from one of the kitchen cabinets and slowly began to fill my beloved baby with plastic beads. The limp shape of my once flattened baby became full once more! My baby was back and better than ever!

Baby Jennifer was my first experience with motherhood. Now that I am grown with a daughter of my own, I know that the love I felt as a child toward my baby doll was nothing compared to the endless love I feel for my precious Juliette.

Don't worry now, baby Jennifer is still loved, she just belongs to my sweet Juliette now. She might be missing a finger and a little worse for wear, but she is still loved and cared for.

Like my mother, I suffered from endometriosis. My road to motherhood was a little bumpy and at times uncertain. I thank God each and every day for the gift of motherhood. I look at the sweet angelic face of my growing girl and I can hardly contain the love that swells within my heart.

The moment my darling daughter was placed in my arms is something I will never forget. Words would not come. I was completely overwhelmed by the array of emotions that I was feeling. I let out a cry of sheer joy and the tears began to fall. What had I done to deserve such a beautiful child?

I love many people, but the love between a mother and child is unlike any other. How do you explain what it feels like to have part of your heart beating outside of your body? To cradle a life that started within your very own? The depth and volume of love I have for my daughter is so overwhelming that at times I am sure that my heart will burst from it.

I always wanted to be a mom, but I had no idea how it would change me. A part of me was awakened on the day that my child was born. A part of me that I never even knew was dormant. There was this whole new side of me just waiting to be let free. I knew instantly that I was born to be a mom.

How can I ever thank God enough for giving me the privilege of not only being *a* mom, but being *her* mom? Being a mother brings me such joy, such purpose, and such pride. Now, not every day is easy. Motherhood is far from simple. There are days when I feel defeated, exhausted, and ill-equipped, but when I lay my sweet girl in her bed at night and she lifts her hands to my face and says, "Momma, I just need to kiss you one more time." My heart melts into one big puddle and I know that there is nothing I would rather be than a mom.

This little girl has taught me so much about love. She has brought my life more meaning than I ever knew existed. In the words of Mildred B. Vermont "Being a full-time mother is one of the highest-salaried jobs... since the payment is pure love."

"I was getting my son ready for his first day of kindergarten when he said to me. 'Mom, I sure hope *they* don't like *them* too much.' I was confused and asked, 'You hope *who* doesn't like *what* too much, honey?' He rolled his eyes, put his hand on his hip, and got that look on his face like it should be obvious to me what he's talking about. Then said in an exasperated tone, 'You know, the *girls*; my *lips*! I just hope the girls don't love my lips too much Mom.' I burst out laughing at how sure he already was at five that every girl wanted to kiss him.

— Kari Day —

The Day I Thought I Couldn't Be a Mom

Raquel Kato

For the first time since my daughter was born, I had one of those days that suddenly stopped me in my tracks. *I don't have what it takes to be a mom,* I thought.

I'm a single mom, I live at home, and I'm so incredibly blessed to have help and support from my extremely selfless family.

The other day I got a glimpse of what it would be like if I was really on my own.

My dad was on a business trip, my brother was on a golf trip, and my mom was working extra late.

I was sick.

Really sick. Head throbbing, high fever, terrible cough, congestion, nausea… just felt awful.

Of course, AvaMarie was also not feeling well. She just cut a tooth and was ready to cut another one, meaning she was *extra* fussy.

After a full day of her being irritable, and me being sick, and getting nothing done (even though I had work projects and a ten-page paper to write for grad school that basically needed to be done that day) you can imagine that I was pretty exhausted and stressed and feeling defeated.

Then AvaMarie started rubbing her eyes early since she missed her nap. *Yes! Finally*, I thought

I took the opportunity to change her and get her ready for bed.

That's when it started.

Blood wrenching screams. Scratching. Kicking.

She was having "a moment."

Only, this "moment" lasted close to two hours.

I couldn't console her. I tried teething tablets, baby Tylenol, rocking, singing, lullaby music, I even nursed her again, and then I tried to play with her thinking she really wasn't tired.

Nothing worked. The tears and screams were flowing full force.

After about twenty minutes, I was already starting to lose my mind. With each scream it felt like someone was hitting my head harder and harder. I had to keep setting AvaMarie down to rush to the bathroom when I felt like I was going to be sick.

By the hour mark of her screaming I couldn't open my eyes anymore because any glimpse of light sent shooting pain through my already aching head.

And then AvaMarie got quiet.

Thank you Jesus.

As I softly slipped her into the crib and tip-toed out of her room, I felt victory.

Then...she wailed.

My heart sank. I couldn't even bring myself to go back in the room just yet. Instead I sat on the floor and started crying along with her.

I was defeated. The devil got to me.

You can't be a mom.

You don't have what it takes.

This is what it would really be like to be a single mom.

You're getting by because you are spoiled, you couldn't do it if you were actually on your own.

Pathetic.

I was in tears. Until I finally dragged myself up and held my poor screaming daughter. Then I texted my mom, *Please come home I need you.*

I sat in the rocking chair rocking my daughter and repeating the Hail Mary over and over and over and over. It seemed like forever, and then my mom came home. By this time AvaMarie was calmed down to just sniffles, but my mom took her and sent me to bed.

A few minutes later, AvaMarie was asleep and my mom was putting a cold washcloth on my forehead, bringing me water, and tucking me into bed. What did I do to deserve such a great mom?

I realized then that she was doing exactly what Jesus has called her to do. Love unconditionally and carrying other's burdens when they can't carry their own.

Galatians 6:2 *"Carry each other's burdens and in this way you may fulfill the law of Christ."*

It's hard to be a single mom. That night I got a glimpse of what it would be like to truly be alone and without help. I'm blessed to have people in my life who are humble enough to help me during this time. There will be a day when I can support myself and live on my own and care for AvaMarie financially, but I will always need support. We all do. Everyone needs help. When the weight is too heavy, we are called to carry each other's burdens. I'm so thankful for my family when they help me through my trials. And I pray that other single moms encounter the love and support I have encountered, because they shouldn't have to do it alone.

My Everything

Lori Cooper

When I was about five years old I had already decided that when I grew up, I was going to be a mother. Starting when I was about eleven years old, I would babysit for the neighbors. I even spent a summer babysitting for a family that had ten children! I adored every minute of it. Children were my calling. When I was in high school I planned on graduating and being a wife and a mother. That's it, that's all I wanted. I did want to work, but I wanted to raise my children and be there with them. That was my priority, number one on my list.

I was graced with four wonderful children and little did I know what childbirth had in store for me. My oldest son, who is now thirty, was born by C-section. He had to stay in the hospital with jaundice for an extra three days. My next child was my daughter, born at thirty-two weeks. She had pneumonia and stayed in the hospital for a couple of weeks. At one point, she was so critical that a Catholic priest gave her the last rights. That is something no mother should have to endure. Fortunately God spared her and she has filled my life with such joy, including two grandsons!

Then my third child, another son, was born premature at twenty-four weeks. I almost lost him too. He spent three months in the hospital. He was born with bleeding on his brain, a hole in his heart, and kidney problems. Again we were blessed, and he survived. He conquered all of these problems. His life has been difficult, but he continues to be an overcomer. Lastly, my youngest son was born at thirty-two weeks. He entered the world with his mother's appendix removal. He spent an extra week in the hospital and came home with a scraped larynx.

I have been asked why I decided to go through all of these pregnancies with all of the risks and all of the complications. Well, because why not? I love my kids; I love the privilege of being their mom. As a mom you fight for your kids, no questions asked. There never was any other option. I would risk my life anytime for my children. The joy of having them is something that no material object on Earth could ever come close to in value or meaning. I see part of me in them, and part of them in their children. I rejoice with them in their happiness, and I suffer with them in their sadness. I pray every night for their safety, their well-being, and their happiness.

Being a mother makes me proud. My children are my everything. My heart swells when my daughter says that she loves me and wants to be the kind of mother to her children that I have been to her. Motherhood is the most rewarding job that there is and the joy that my children and grandchildren have brought me makes my life worth living and gives me the strength to carry on in both the good times and the bad.

"My daughter has dubbed her daddy a 'Fancy Man.' When asked what makes him fancy, she said, 'Because he doesn't talk about poop and farts.'"

— Rachael Moshman —

Worth the Wait
Jennifer Daiker

"If you were supposed to have kids you would have them naturally" was a common response when people first heard that my husband and I chose to adopt. These comments were tucked in-between the usual "Why can't you have children?" and "Have you tried?"

The process was long and hard. Our first meeting with our selected agency was with a room full of other hopefuls looking for quick answers to getting a baby. We didn't realize this meeting would define the struggles and wait times we would endure throughout the process. We were handed a packet outlining what our lives would look like for the next nine months to two years. It was meant to scare those unwilling to dedicate their lives for a child and for several, it worked. For my husband and I, it ignited a fire underneath us and allowed us the dedication required to accept the challenge and reach our dream of becoming parents.

We filled out the paperwork, attended the classes, and allowed social workers to invade our privacy; all with the promise that we would eventually be chosen by a potential birth-mother and that the match would be perfect, and we would know instantly that they were the one.

That day took twenty-one months of heartache and disappointment.

Nothing prepares you for a journey of ups and downs. Our reason for adopting was a medical one. We aren't martyrs or heroes, much to people's surprise. We were a couple in the next stage of our lives. Unlike pregnant women, when you pass each stage through adoption there is no belly growth showing your progress.

In fact, it becomes more apparent that this is the one major difference in your life. The struggles, though often small, seem huge in the moment. You say you're adopting and it feels as if everyone is getting pregnant around you. You've sent your opportunity book to a potential birth-mother and feel as if she's the one...only to find out she isn't. You are matched with a birth-mother and then your gut tells you that you're being scammed.

Not getting pregnant sucks. Knowing you can't get pregnant even when people say "You need to pray harder" or "It'll happen" doesn't ease the pain. It infuriates you because you're not being heard. Working countless hours on selling yourself with a ten to twenty page book that isn't well received, breaks your heart. You thought you'd be chosen for that perfect baby and now someone else gets him or her. Your matching period should be joyous, but the stress of the unknown and the flakiness kills you.

One thing we found most frustrating was feeling duped and realizing that stereotype does exist with adoption. Several families are scammed. The adoptive couples wear their hearts on their sleeves and their dream of becoming parents seems so close. Some birth-mothers feed off that and it is the driving force for free rent, utilities, and clothing. All that hard-earned money from the couple that should have gone to the right birth-mother is instead gone to a scam artist and then the couple must begin all over again.

This is not all birth-mothers! This is the stereotype featured in Lifetime movies: scared adoptive couples and their friends reminding them of the risk they are taking. Those friends don't realize that if given the choice, you'd have your own but God has other plans.

After months of receiving no bites off of our opportunity book, my husband and I went back to the drawing board. We discovered that the tips our agency gave us, made us seem less reachable by the younger mothers that would be our perfect fit. I, in my mid-twenties and my husband, just turned thirty, really needed to connect with someone young. The change made all the difference, an opportunity came up within weeks and we were officially matched.

She wasn't the right one for us. She was a great stepping stone in understanding the feeling we were desperate for. She was in her mid-twenties and though we felt excitement at the opportunity, it didn't change the fact that when we spoke on the phone there wasn't the instant connection we'd hoped for. Saying no to that opportunity was one of the hardest decisions we ever had to make. However the end game was so perfect that it really holds true when your social worker says "When the right one comes along, you'll know. The first match just wasn't your baby."

Our perfect match was a nineteen-year-old girl. She was thirty-five weeks along and, up to that point, prepared to raise the child on her own. She lived with her mom, her sister, and her niece. She realized she had so much love for her little girl but no means of support to give her the life she'd dreamed of. Her mother had mentioned adoption a few times, and at thirty-five weeks, the birth-mother felt that if she could find the perfect family she'd want to give her baby girl a better life. She requested an open adoption and a lunch meeting which made us front runners.

The day we had declined our first match the social worker drove back to the agency to grab our book for this eager girl. We are so glad she did because that same afternoon we received a call that the girl had decided we were her perfect match and she wanted to meet us. All the sorrow and heartache vanished and endless possibilities opened up.

Our first meeting was much like a first date. My husband and I were nervous and elated, dying to meet her and hoping to be liked. Our palms sweat as we waited in anticipation. When they walked through the door with their social worker, we could feel the nerves fade as the joy on everyone's face filled the restaurant. Everyone talked about what they wanted from this situation and how they wanted to see the baby girl grow.

It was heartwarming to know that we would one day unite our families and give this future little girl so much love.

Upon the first meeting we had mere weeks to go and that allowed for little time to get to know one another, but we managed to make it work. We visited on weekends, and when the day finally arrived we joined the birth-mother and her family at the hospital. A scheduled C-section allowed all of us to be there until we heard news of her new arrival.

She was breathtaking. She was everything my husband and I had hoped for and more. The moment she was born we felt a kindred connection with her.

Now, in each state the law works differently for adoptive couples and the birth parents. In Texas, where we reside, the baby is in possession of the birth-mother for forty-eight hours in which she'll have the option to change her mind. This is both terrifying and understandable. Though the forty-eight hours seemed unbearable, we all knew what we had come together to do—raise this beautiful baby girl.

When my husband and I sat outside the room after those stressed out forty-eight hours—for all of us—and gave the family privacy as they signed their rights away, my heart broke. The emotional roller coaster we endured not only for those two days but for the last twenty-one months came rushing in. The sadness I felt for them was something I hadn't expected. They loved her *so* much that they knew she needed a better life than what both the birth-mother and birth-father could offer. They trusted us enough to care for this little gem that they made and loved for nine months. What an honor and a privilege to be trusted with something so sacred to this world.

I know several people who never truly understood the bond of a birth-mother and an adoptive mother, but it is third in line for love. I have my husband and my daughter and then I have the birth-mother who gave us a life we couldn't give ourselves. We will forever be thankful and appreciative of the little girl she brought into our lives and the family that came with her.

For those in a predicament where nerves, stress, and confusion reside, start to make a plan. Our family doesn't believe that the birth-mother gave up her child, she made a plan to allow her little girl the financial support she couldn't offer. Adoption is a wonderful option and without people willing to carry the child to term and pass along a treasure, my husband and I would still have a missing piece to our family puzzle.

"'I have to go potty' my three-year-old son declared as we neared the library. I parked the car and we quickly made our way across the lawn as I noticed that only my daughter was with me. Turning I froze, as I saw my mischievous son standing in the grass, pants down (bare bottom facing the busy street behind us) as he relieved himself on the library's lawn. My daughter was mortified, pretended not to know him as she quickened her pace and advised me to do the same, which I might have...maybe."

— Celi Camacho —

It's Not Always Planned, But It Is Meant to Be

Jessica Ward

Becoming a mother has been by far the most life changing experience I have ever gone through. It has changed every aspect of my life and has taught me so much about life, love, and priorities. Perhaps the biggest thing I have learned from motherhood is that that you shouldn't try to control everything, not everything will go as planned, but it will go as it should.

I found out that I was pregnant one day while I was at work. Ironic though it is, I had just been talking to a friend the previous day about how I wasn't sure if I could even have kids because I didn't ovulate regularly. I woke up the next morning, and I just had a feeling. I can't explain exactly what the feeling was, but I like to think of it as mother's intuition starting early. During my lunch break, I went out and purchased a pregnancy test. Waiting for the results seemed like an eternity. It was the longest two minutes of my life. Two lines popped up and my mind raced with so many thoughts. This was definitely not a planned pregnancy. The timing was not ideal, I guess I should have been nervous or a little uneasy, but really I was just so happy. It felt amazing to know that I was pregnant. I was going to be a mom!

I had always wanted to start a family the traditional way. I wanted to be married, I wanted to have already finished school, and I imagined myself already having a successful career. At the time I found out I was expecting, I was in a committed relationship but not married, I only had my associates degree, and I worked part time. I was determined to not let my pregnancy hold me back. In fact, knowing that I was going to be responsible for taking care of a precious new life only inspired me to be better and do better.

Once I became a mother, I had such determination to finish my degree. I am actively pursuing my bachelor's and am taking more classes than before. You could even say I am excelling academically. I have someone else to worry about besides myself, so I am no longer just moving along at a leisurely pace. Becoming a mother was just the kick-in-the-butt I needed to get myself through college before the age of thirty.

Once finding out about my baby, I became a research addict and a complete health nut. I no longer wanted to eat processed foods. I fed myself and my baby only the best. I planned to breastfeed and was determined to have an all-natural child birth. This pregnancy pushed me in the right direction. It inspired me to become a healthier woman in every respect.

I was pretty fortunate and had a fairly smooth pregnancy. I did have morning sickness that wanted to be my best friend. It hung around all day, but I didn't care. I had this amazing blessing growing inside of me so as far as I was concerned, it was all well worth it. Once I hit thirty-four weeks gestation, things took a downhill stroll. I started having protein in my urine, and my blood pressure was high. I was labeled high-risk and put on bed rest. I'm not sure how much rest I got between my weekly OB appointments and twice-weekly high-risk OB appointments, but it's what the doctors ordered so it's what I did. This certainly was not how I planned for my pregnancy to go, but as long as my baby was safe then I was content.

Once I hit thirty-six weeks, I went to my high-risk doctor and almost didn't pass the testing. My son had not moved during the stress test and almost didn't move during the sonogram test. Luckily, he passed the sonogram test and I was able to leave. We went out to lunch before going to my regular OB appointment. We arrived at my OB's office and she did her usual routine. She noticed that my blood pressure was way too high and stepped out of the room for a few minutes. I started to get really nervous. She came back in and asked me to come into her office. My mind started racing. Once in her office, she explained that she wanted to take my baby that day...*take*?!? No no no! That was not at all what I wanted, not at all what I was prepared for.

I wanted an all-natural birth, I wanted delayed cord clamping, I wanted skin-to-skin, I wanted to catch my own baby. My mind continued to race. I had three loads of laundry at home to put away, my bag wasn't packed, my dog was at home and needed to be taken to my grandmother's, I wanted my car to be cleaned before putting my newborn in it, his crib needed to be set up. None of that mattered though; my baby was ready to come.

The doctor explained that my liver functions were being affected and in order to get rid of these potentially dangerous side effects, we had to get the baby out. With my blood pressure being so high and my body under so much stress, she advised me not to deliver the baby naturally since this would only increase my blood pressure and put my body under more stress. The birth I planned would simply be too dangerous for both me and my baby. It might not have been my plan, but it was what needed to be done.

Throughout my pregnancy, I knew that I wanted to breastfeed my son. There was no denying the amazing effects that it has for both mom and baby. With him being early, it was hard for him to suck. I used the breast pump for extra stimulation and would put the colostrum on a spoon and feed it to him. I wanted to make sure that he got every bit of that liquid gold. My son had jaundice and the nurses suggested that I give him some formula to make him poop more. So I did. I didn't want to, but once again, not everything goes as planned. I would pump while he ate so I still got the stimulation. I decided it was better for both of us for me to pump and feed. He was considered premature and would tire out after trying to latch and therefore wouldn't eat. I never was able to exclusively breastfeed, and it started to wear on me. When my son was three months old, I had to return to work. It was the hardest thing I have ever done. It felt like a part of me was missing. My milk supply slowly went down to where I was only pumping four ounces per day. At that point my son needed six-ounce bottles. I would have terrible thoughts of how I wasn't good enough to provide nourishment for my own son. What kind of mother couldn't even feed her child? I felt so guilty. My heart broke.

I had to look on the bright side and remain positive. I was able to give my son mostly breast milk for the first three months of his life. I tried very hard. I did the best I could, and my son would be healthy regardless. I decided that it was best for me to quit pumping. It would help keep me from feeling down on myself, and I could spend the time it took to pump playing with my son instead. It all worked out for the best.

After having my son I can say that one thing did go as planned. He is healthy, and he is happy. He has shown me a whole new depth of love. He has taught me that things that once seemed so important are no longer necessary. Who knew that it was not an absolute necessity to shower every day, or that you can actually shower, shave, and brush your teeth in under twelve minutes? I no longer need to go out with my friends as frequently. Sitting at home with my little family is just as (if not more) enjoyable. These are the memories that I will cherish for the rest of my life. I can't wait to teach him everything he wants to know.

As he gets older, I will explain to him that sometimes you just need to let go of things that don't matter. What will be, will be. If something is meant to happen then it will. It may not be what you had planned, but it will be what is best and what is right. Sometimes the best thing to do is to simply relax. Don't stress or worry over silly things. Becoming a mother is without a doubt the best thing that has ever happened to me. I cannot imagine my life without this blessing. Life has a newfound meaning and is more beautiful than ever.

"My daughter once asked me 'Mom, which apps did you play with when you

were a little girl?'

I laughed a little, thought about it, and said, 'Atari.'"

— Donna Brzykcy —

His Grace Heals

Lee U.
co-written by Jillian Amodio

My story starts like so many others, buried in my past. I grew up in a faith-minded family. We loved our church, and we loved each other. Our home was close enough to our church that I grew up walking there with my family each Sunday.

My happy life was shattered when my father died unexpectedly when I was only fifteen years old. I was angry, I was lost, and my faith fell to the wayside. I was angry with God. How could I love the same God who took my dad? I wanted nothing to do with faith or God. I turned my back on Him. Thankfully He never turns His on us.

Before my story got better though, it got worse…much, much worse.

At sixteen years old, still dealing with the sudden loss of my father, I was sexually abused by my high school teacher for over a year. This event set off a series of bad decisions and led me down a path paved with confusion and poor judgment which ultimately ended with heartache that was deeper than any I had ever experienced.

I became a wild child. I was promiscuous and reckless. I experimented with drugs and abused alcohol. I was truly a lost soul on my way to destruction and despair.

At twenty-one years of age, I found myself in an all too familiar situation. I was involved in yet another emotionally abusive relationship with a separated but still married man. I wanted to end it. I felt alone and unloved. He wanted me to stay. I was torn.

I found myself pregnant with his child. I had been raised in a Christian household. Even though I was raised a Christian, matters of sex, chastity, and what it meant to be truly pro-life were never discussed. Deep down I knew abortion was wrong, but I couldn't see another way out. I needed a solution, I was desperate. I never even told my mom.

On the day of my scheduled abortion, I went alone. I sat in a cold, lonely, unforgiving office. I was led to an equally cold, lonely, and unforgiving procedure room. I lay on the table and I cried. I cried inconsolable tears of anger, hurt, despair, and heartache. The emotional torment I experienced after the abortion had been completed was unlike any other. No one tells you how empty and destroyed you feel. No one prepares you for the void that you feel in the depth of your heart. This kind of pain never leaves you. Time heals as much as it can, but the pain remains permanently etched into your heart. You never stop feeling like something, someone, is missing.

This was the darkest part of my life. I was broken, lost, empty.

A year later, my life started to take a turn in the right direction. I began to see a light at the end of my broken road. My heart began to heal and my faith was starting to be restored.

I married my now husband. The same boy I had known all my life; the one who had had a crush on me since we were thirteen. He brought me out of the shadows and showed me that the sun could shine on the broken pieces.

When my husband and I got pregnant with our first child, who will always be my second, I called the father of my first child and apologized. I apologized for the lost chance at being a father; I apologized for ending the life of our child before it truly had a chance to begin.

Throughout my second pregnancy I kept thinking, *She should have an older sibling.* I was thrilled and excited to be bringing a new life into this world, but at the same time I was still mourning the life that had been lost.

Ultimately my husband was the reason I began to heal from the wounds and scars my abortion had inflicted. After our marriage, I started to go to church with him. My faith in God began to resurface. It felt like I was coming home.

The day that I officially joined the Catholic church, I found out that the teacher who had abused me in high school was arrested. All of the broken pieces started to fall back into place. God had me cradled in His almighty hands, and I could feel His loving presence molding me back into the woman He created me to be.

In the span of just a couple of years, I had married the man of my dreams, joined the church, found closure to my abuse, and been gifted with another pregnancy.

Whereas my first pregnancy killed my spirit, my second brought me back. Life was glorious and I truly understood that God is good. I still struggled for a few years with my abuse and I still seek help in the form of counseling to deal with my past.

I now have five beautiful children. With my first two children, I could not nurse them. It was impossible for me, considering my past, to separate the sexual aspect from the nurturing aspect. Finally, with the birth of my third child, I was able to do the job my body was created to do. I felt comfortable and whole with my role as a mother.

I strive daily to instill values such as chastity, purity, and dignity in my children. We home school and talk about anything and everything. Our house is filled with love and acceptance. It took me a while to understand how great and forgiving our God is. But once I understood that, my life took on a new meaning. Even now when my children do wrong, I have one rule to their punishment. The minute they go to confession, their punishment is lifted. If God has forgiven their transgression, then how could I possibly carry on with a punishment? God's forgiveness heals.

I have yet to tell my children about my abortion. I have not quite found a way to approach that topic. I don't know when or if I will tell them, but one thing is for sure. My children are being raised to know that their parents will never turn their backs on them. Should they ever find themselves in a difficult or compromising situation, all they need to do is come to us and we will help them through whatever difficulties they are facing.

God is so good and He has gifted us with the most precious gift there is: the gift of family.

Well Done Mom
Stephanie Page

Try it, I know you'll like it.

That is how I feel about being a mom.

Whether you are in your teens, twenties, or forties.

Married, dating, victim of rape, or dealing with the consequences of a one night stand.

A career woman, high school student, or wandering.

If you find yourself pregnant, by whatever circumstance, follow through. It's worth it.

As I write this my two month old baby girl is lying next to me. This precious bundle was created inside my body, I nourished and grew her. She is mine. A product of me. Placed inside me, created for a purpose.

I have three girls, and each pregnancy was different just as each child is different. My first we got pregnant without trying. My second we miscarried before we were gifted with another. My third we tried to get pregnant for almost a year. Each baby is a precious gift created and placed on this Earth for that time in that place. Babies are no accident. Just like you and I have a purpose, so do our children. From the moment of their first flutter in our womb, they are working out God's plan for their lives. I am convinced that part of His plan for children is how having them changes their mothers.

Whether we have them for nine months, five minutes, or the rest of our lives, being a mother changes us so that we are never the same.

Maybe today you're expecting because of a situation of lust or misplaced passion. Maybe that baby has been placed in your womb because you were misused and mistreated. You wonder why God has done this to you, has allowed this to happen.

Because He brings beauty from ashes.

He makes that which is ugly beautiful.

He is the great redeemer.

A baby is always beautiful.

Children are the way we leave our legacies. They are our mark made on the world. Our children carry on our values, our stories, our love.

Being a mom is the hardest thing I have ever done and ever will do, and without God's help I would be lost.

Our Creator is our ally as we mother. You and I are not capable on our own to grow, raise, and shape a life, but He who calls you is faithful. As we lean on Him, He equips us for the task.

No matter who you are and how you found yourself with child, welcome to motherhood. We moms have to stick together. I am with you in spirit and as you welcome that precious baby I want you to hear, "How beautiful. Well done. Mom."

And know you're not alone.

"'How do all your body parts stay on?' I was asked one day.

I went with skin."

— Morgan, @the818 —

The Daisy Pin:
How Grief Gave Way to Joy
Rachael Moshman

One moment I was lying in bed, calmly reading a novel. Then the main character became pregnant and I snapped. I got up and searched through my jewelry box for the pointiest pin I could find. I pulled out a large, vintage yellow daisy pin. I grabbed the condoms from the night table and started poking holes in them. Poke, poke, poke. Jab, jab, jab. The pin was too large and left big, gaping, noticeable holes. Just like the ones I felt inside of me.

Looking at those holes in the silver wrapper was a big wake-up call for me. I hid the condoms under tissues in the bathroom garbage can, sat back on the bed, and sobbed. I'd been hiding my feelings for so long. I hadn't allowed myself time to mourn or grieve. The pain couldn't be held back any longer and came out in a big ball of crazy condom poking.

I had experienced a miscarriage several months before. The pregnancy wasn't planned. In fact, babies weren't in the plan at all. My husband made it clear from the beginning that he didn't want children. I told him that I was willing to sacrifice babies for him. I actually thought he'd change his mind. He didn't and I struggled with letting go of my strong desire to have a child.

We were in a really stressful place about six years into our marriage. We were trying to sell a house in a market where no one was biting, after feeling forced to vacate it due to harassments and threats from the people across the street. We were living in an empty home owned by my mother-in-law until our house sold and provided us with the funds to buy again. We weren't happy living there and the situation created all kinds of family drama. Finances were tight. My husband was a full-time student. His father was extremely ill. We were stressed to the max. I forgot to take my birth control pill for three days.

I was sure the exhaustion, headaches, and nausea were from the stress. I thought stress was also what was delaying my period and that my breasts were so incredibly sore because of PMS. I assumed I was having a bad reaction to my toothpaste when I threw up several mornings in a row. Being pregnant didn't even cross my mind. Sex was scarce during that time, so I didn't think much of it. Plus, I'd missed doses here and there in the past without a problem.

Then I woke up in the night and a pool of blood hit the floor the moment I stood up. Pregnancy still didn't enter my head. I thought my period had to be extra strong because it was late. I called my gynecologist the next day when the heavy bleeding continued. The doctor called it a "missed pregnancy."

I was numb and in shock. I stayed in bed crying and eating chocolate peanut butter ice cream for a few days, but I didn't fully deal with my feelings. I shoved them down. I went back to work. I pretended I was okay. I told myself I was fine.

I wasn't fine. Women who are handling things "fine" don't poke holes in condoms. I was a mess. My husband was sad when he learned of the miscarriage, but it was only because he knew I was hurting. He was relieved there would be no baby and was terrified pregnancy would occur again. I finally realized that he wasn't going to change his mind. No matter how much he adored me, he did not want a baby.

Would I have actually gone through with using the condoms if the holes weren't so big and noticeable? I like to think I wouldn't, but I don't know for sure. I'm glad the holes were so glaring. It forced me to stop what I was doing and to acknowledge my grief and pain.

I opened up to my husband about all the feelings swirling around inside. I wasn't just mourning the loss of my pregnancy, but the hope of any future pregnancies. I felt so ripped off, like the universe was playing a cruel joke by allowing me to get pregnant, but then miscarrying before even getting the chance to be happy or excited about the prospect of motherhood.

We talked and talked. The conversation kept coming up again and again for months. I had a lot to process. Through these talks two big points became clear: My husband wasn't totally opposed to being a father, he just didn't want a baby; I just wanted to be a mother and how it happened actually wasn't important to me.

We'd thrown around the possibility of older child adoption for years, but never seriously talked about it prior to this. We started to really consider it. We made it a tentative "some day" plan. I dove into research. I was shocked when I told my husband about upcoming classes to get licensed to adopt from the foster care system and he said, "Let's sign up."

A year after we officially started the process, our daughter moved in with us. She was nine years old and had been in foster care for five years. She had suffered abuse, neglect, poverty, homelessness, abandonment, instability, and many other things children should not have to face. We finalized the adoption six months later.

Parenting a traumatized child is challenging, but it is also so very rewarding. Our daughter has made huge progress since coming home to us. She's learning to control her anger, work through her feelings and trust us. I felt a pull to her from the moment I saw a photo of her sweet face. She is my daughter. My baby. I was made to be her mother. My husband is an amazing father. Nothing brings me more joy than watching the two of them laugh together. She has healed me. She has completed me. The holes in my heart were waiting for her to fill them.

"My ten-year-old grandson, Chase, really got me good one day. The sad thing is he wasn't trying to insult me, he was being sincere. I've been addicted to yard sales for years. My latest treasure, a vintage horse saddle with a lasso, was a steal I got for only $5. I just couldn't resist. My latest purchase led to this compliment. 'This is so cool. Grandma when I grow up, I want to be a hoarder just like you!'

I am embarrassed, but I'm really not a hoarder."

— Sheila Atkins —

My Children; My Life
Amy Stoddard
co-written by Jillian Amodio

Wow, where to start. Have you ever felt certain that you knew where your life was headed only to find yourself living a life you never could have imagined?

I was sixteen years old when I found out that I was pregnant with my first child. My Megan. I had been dating her father for only three months. He was the first person I had ever had sex with, and I never imagined I would end up pregnant. I remember being scared, but not panicked. I was honestly more scared of telling my mother that I was pregnant than actually being pregnant. My mother is a wonderful Christian woman. Growing up we wore long dresses; we went to church; we lived by the rules. She was a God-fearing woman and in our family getting pregnant outside of marriage was a huge deal.

When I told my mom, she was sad, but she was always supportive from day one. "We are going to do this together," she said. She went to the pregnancy clinic with me and I remember when the lady came in and confirmed the pregnancy test, she handed my mom a box of tissues. My mom's first words were "You are not aborting this baby."

I relied on my family for affirmation that I was doing the right thing. Fortunately they were more supportive than I ever could have hoped for. Once the news was out, everyone just rallied around me with love.

Despite being scared and a little confused, I can honestly say that looking back I never felt like I couldn't handle my situation. I felt that I was right where I needed to be and everything would turn out ok.

Of course there were times when I was plagued by uncertainty, but a little bit of faith goes a really long way.

Chad, the father said to me, "There is no way we can do this. We are sixteen years old, we cannot have a baby." I will not say that I never thought of not having the baby, I just knew that I could never forgive myself if I ended the life of my child. As far as I was concerned, we had caused this, and we would deal with whatever consequences came with it. Even if I had the baby, I could never give her up. From the moment I found out I was pregnant, I felt that this baby was mine and I was going to keep her.

Because Chad and I had only been dating for a few months, I never even knew how much longer it would last. Would we date two more days? Two more weeks? Two more years? I really didn't know. I did know, regardless, that I was going to care for and love this baby.

Throughout my pregnancy and even after my daughter was born, there were plenty of people telling me I couldn't do this. "You're so young." "How are you going to handle a baby." Everyone had something to say.

I was determined to make it work, and I did just that.

From the minute my daughter was born any fear or worry disappeared. Holding her, having her, loving her; it all felt so natural. Yes I was young, but I felt like I had been born for this. I was born to be a mother.

Megan was born in September. I finished my senior year of high school through home schooling after my daughter was born. For six weeks I had a nurse come to my house and ensure that my education was completed. My mom was right there with me encouraging me to carry on with school.

I had always wanted to be a teacher, but once Megan was born I just felt like I needed to do something different, something a little quicker. I knew I would love being a nurse, so my school counselor helped me find the perfect program. In eighteen months I was a licensed practical nurse! Megan was going on two years old, I was working part time, and my family was helping with childcare.

I had saved enough money to afford to move me and Megan out on our own. We were still living with my parents, and while I valued my mom's support, my dad was an alcoholic and I did not want my daughter raised in that type of environment. She was nearly three when we had our own apartment.

Chad and I stayed together until Megan was about five years old, until we both realized that the only reason we were together was because we had a child. We were not doing each other any justice. It got to the point where we were fighting all the time and we needed to end things for the sake of everyone's happiness. It really wasn't that difficult considering the fact that we never even lived together. He went away to a four year college and continued with his life while I was home by myself raising the baby.

A year after Chad and I separated, I met my future husband. My James. I had two more beautiful children with him during the course of our marriage, Makenzie and Jay. He accepted Megan as his own, and we quickly became one happy family. James was in the military, and I adjusted to being a military wife.

While we did have a few happy years together, sadly that was not my happy ending. My husband was killed in combat. My world crashed down around me. My life caved in. I could not imagine how I was going to carry on. Here I was once again a single mom, this time with three small children.

I relied on my family, my faith, and of course my children to get me through the pain and heartache of our unspeakable loss. I saw the tears running down their faces and the pain that had been etched into their hearts, and I knew that I needed to pull myself together for the sake of their happiness. My babies did not deserve to live in despair. My children needed to remember what happiness felt like, and it was my job to remind them.

I picked up the pieces and began to rebuild our life together. I poured my heart and soul into making my children happy and making sure that their lives were complete and that they knew how loved they were.

With each smile that appeared on their faces, each hug we gave, each kiss goodnight, my heart started to heal right along with theirs. A few years later God blessed me yet again with another wonderful man, Tony. He took away a little bit more of my pain and loneliness. He has helped support me and my children and together we have become a family. There will always be a place in my heart for James. He is gone but will never be forgotten. He is still a big part of my children's life. We visit his gravesite and talk about him freely.

Our family expanded even more when Tony and I welcomed Charlie into our lives. With the birth of our son, my fourth child, I once again experienced the healing that new life can bring. There is nothing in the world that gives me greater pleasure than being a mom.

Our little boy was perfect. He was exactly what our family needed. As Charlie got older however, it became clear that something was wrong. He was delayed and the doctors were concerned. After countless appointments, tests, and evaluations, our Charlie was diagnosed with Sensory Processing Disorder. Until my child was diagnosed with it, I knew nothing about it. With his early diagnosis we have gotten him into early intervention programs and he has begun to thrive.

Some days are better than others. There are days when nothing I do can get him to calm down, he hits, he throws tantrums, he gets frustrated. My heart breaks when I see the frustration on his face, I want so badly to help him process what is going on around him. Having a child with special needs has taught me more about love than I ever knew there was to know.

The love of a child cannot be compared. My children are the reason I breathe each day. They are my heart and soul. Without them my life would be meaningless. My life has been far from easy, but I have been abundantly blessed. God is so good to those who trust in Him and my children have been proof of that. As I look back on my whole life, I have come to realize that each step has been placed there for a reason, to mold me into the person I am today. I would not change a thing.

I Gave Up
Hillary Gould

I gave up my career.

I gave up my hometown.

I gave up my longtime friends.

When my husband proposed to me, we decided that children were so important that they needed to be nurtured and cared for every day by their mother. At the time, I was teaching in the public school, the exact job that I'd dreamed of since I was a child; I was a twenty-three-year-old woman who had lived in the same small town since birth; all of my friends were there. I left all of that behind to go start my own family. It was not easy, and many times I wondered if I'd made the right decision to give up all of those things. However, I did gain some new things.

I have gained a son who wants to retell every word of every book he reads to *me*.

I have gained a second son who hurries to hold my hand whenever we walk anywhere together.

I have gained a daughter who thinks that Mommy and Girl time is the best thing in the world.

I have gained lots of hugs and kisses and "I love you, Mommy's."

I have gained a love like no other. Unconditional love exists from my children to me, and from me to my children.

I gave up many things, but the blessings of motherhood are so much more than anything I ever gave up. Being a mother is not always easy. During my first pregnancy, a fifteen-pound ovarian cyst was discovered.

Emergency surgery had to be done to remove the cyst while my child was in my belly too. Pre-term labor (which was stopped) and kidney infections followed, until my baby was born three weeks early—a very healthy, beautiful baby boy! My second pregnancy was uncomplicated and full-term. However, during labor, my baby's heartbeat started to decrease. The baby had to be delivered quickly. After my second baby boy was born, he was grunting, but not crying and barely breathing. He had to be in NICU for eight days, but is now handsome and healthy. My third pregnancy was again uncomplicated, the birth was uncomplicated, and my baby girl cried as soon as she was delivered (neither of my boys did this, so that was a beautiful sound to hear). However, she inherited a condition from me called polysyndactyly, which means that multiple fingers and/or toes are webbed. She had fingers and toes webbed and also had an extra toe on each foot (as did I). She had to have several surgeries to correct the problem, and with a family history of malignant hypothermia (relatives have died due an allergic reaction to the medication that is used to put them to sleep for surgery), this was an added stress to my being a new mom. As the children grow, there are also difficult experiences. Discipline issues, potty training, and teaching them to do other tasks on their own are not easy.

However, despite all that I have given up and all of the difficulties throughout my pregnancies nothing matches all of the things that I have gained through becoming a mother. It is truly the greatest calling in my life. I treasure the moments with my children. They are blessings to me and make my life more than it could have ever been without them.

"When my son was eight years old, he was afraid of old people. He thought they were a rowdy bunch and associated them with loud music and speeding cars all because of the cars with messages that said things like *Senior's Rule!*"

— Shirley Bailey —

Momma Wanna-Be
Carla Rogers

Watching *Full House* used to bring me such laughter and joy. But now, as I watch little Michelle Tanner toddle around, tears flow. I don't mean just a knot in my throat and a lone tear down my cheek. I mean sobs that come from the depths of a soul that has almost given up. It is not in my control whether to bawl or how loud I sob, so I have relegated myself to only watching these family shows in the comfort of my own house, in a room far away from my beloved husband.

It wasn't always like this. In fact during the first years of our marriage, I couldn't see myself with a baby. We weren't young'uns when we married, but that usual drive for a child wasn't there. It didn't bother me at all when all our friends had baby showers. Picking out toys and clothes for the precious bundles was so much fun. But in the process of time our friends became grandparents, which bothered me. A slow burning ache was ignited in my soul.

Then I hit forty. Everything changed. That strong maternal urge I had heard about all my life kicked in. And it came bucking like a rodeo horse. I saw children everywhere we went. And I wanted one. My heart broke, longing to hear the word Momma from my own child.

Mother's Day at church was a killer. All the mothers made the trek up the aisle to receive a gift. All the children ran out, excited, with gifts in their chubby little hands. Seeing the mother's faces glow as their little darlings handed them their special handmade gifts felt like a thousand daggers in my heart. Oh, how I dreaded Mother's Day. I still do.

But it wasn't God's plan—yet. About this time, my parents started to fail in health. Since I am an only child, we spent the next five years taking care of them, with no thought of children. We were happy to put our lives on hold for them, since they had done so much for us through the years. Many sleepless nights over my parents' health brought many regretful thoughts. One was that my parents would never have the grandchildren they so patiently waited for. They never complained or hinted for us to hurry up and give them grandchildren, but I knew they wanted a grandchild almost as much as they wanted me.

After both my parents died, that dang maternal urge came back stronger than ever. That is when I started crying at anything that looked like my ideal family, one with kids. The ideal family that I thought I would never have. I started thinking that God was very cruel to wait until this late in my life to give me the overwhelming desire to have kids since I didn't see a way, naturally, that this would ever happen. The natural way of having children was out because of certain health issues. I guess we also were waiting for the perfect time, but then life got in the way.

Tired of feeling so depressed, I decided to call our state Department of Social Services to learn our options for adoption. In my mind, DSS would gently let me know that we were too old. Then my desire would go away with all options having been researched to the fullest degree. No one our age adopts, do they? DSS answered this with a resounding yes. Many couples go through the process to gain custody of family members. Some of these couples are grandparents, some are uncles and aunts. We met many of these couples in our classes. But there were others, just like us.

All through the process, I was afraid to tell people that we were adopting—not for fear of their reaction but fear that the adoption wouldn't be approved. I was so scared to get my hopes up that I didn't want to get others' hopes up as well. When we did let others in on our plans, we received all kinds of reactions. Some people said we were too old and set in our ways. "You know what will happen, as soon as you adopt you will end up pregnant" is another one we heard a lot.

If people knew how our hearts broke every time we see them with their children, if they could see how desperately we wanted what they had, then maybe they wouldn't say things like that. And if we did get pregnant, I would never want our adopted child to think they were any less a part of our family because they were adopted. I will never understand why people assume that every family has to have a blood connection to be a family.

In one class, they asked each of us to describe our ideal child, even though we all knew that wouldn't happen. I almost couldn't squeak out my answer, the knot in my throat kept getting bigger and bigger. I felt the tears coming—fear that this dearly held dream would never come true—but I certainly didn't want to sob before a whole room full of strangers. So I softly related my few thoughts and gave my husband a pleading look to take his turn. I couldn't shake the feeling that this adoption would never happen.

In the following months, we passed all the DSS requirements. The official approval for adoption was finally ours. Believe it or not, I didn't know whether to be thrilled beyond the stars or be fearful of what would happen next. Petrified that my last hope of having a child would be taken away even at this late stage, I told very few people.

Then what I had dreaded happened. Within a couple of weeks of getting our approval, I became unemployed. Our adoption is still on, but even if the perfect child was found, we wouldn't be able to afford him. I know the saying, "If you wait until you can afford children, you will never have them," but we can't even afford ourselves at the moment.

I pray every day that God protects the child that He has for us. I have faith that our adoption will go through, eventually. This is just a side road God has in store for us. For any mother-to-be that is in the process of deciding whether to give their precious baby up for adoption, remember this story of a mother-wanna-be who would love to love your little bundle.

"Making a decision to have a child—it's momentous. It is to decide forever to have your heart go walking around outside your body."

— Elizabeth Stone, author —

Treasures of the Heart
Celi Camacho

My husband and I were what everyone called "meant to be." What started with friendship developed into a beautiful love story and I married the love of my life. That being said, our life was far from perfect, but it was ours to go through together and here we are seventeen years later. Two years into our marriage we were ready to start a family. Did I say ready? Actually I was petrified but felt my clock ticking away.

I was thirty-two when I got pregnant with my first child. I was excited and nervous all at once realizing that I was standing at the threshold of motherhood. I had my doubts because although I was in my thirties I still had moments when I felt like a kid myself. I had heard so many horror stories about pregnancy and painful deliveries that I was fearful of the unknown. As my pregnancy progressed I was constantly sick to the point that instead of gaining weight I actually lost fifteen pounds. Forget morning sickness, I had all day sickness. You would think that I was miserable but the truth is the complete opposite. Yes my body was changing and nausea did take over, but the moment I felt that life growing inside me, moving and kicking, all I could focus on was how amazing I felt. I hadn't met her yet but had already fallen completely in love with her. Being pregnant was the most amazing feeling I had ever had. There was nothing to compare it to because it was so unique. I loved being pregnant so much so that on a particular night I started having contractions and had a bit of a panic attack because I wasn't ready to stop being pregnant. I didn't want to give up that beautiful feeling. I think that somewhere in my mind I thought I was doing something *so* important, something that would make a difference. I had never felt that important before. It turned out to be Braxton Hicks and I was so happy to know that I could be pregnant for a little bit longer.

A few weeks later contractions came again, this time I was ready and eager to meet my baby. On December 18th, 1998 my beautiful daughter was born and I was never the same. How can you describe a heart so full that it overflows? I was now in that club, you know that one where you get to say "you'll understand when you're a mom." It's so true! The minute I held her for the first time I experienced an overwhelming flood of emotions that I had never experienced before. There she was with her red puffy cheeks and sweet trusting eyes and she was mine. True, I had to share her with my husband, but she was mine. I was in heaven.

I was determined to breastfeed and therefore did not sleep. This little six pound baby girl always wanted to feed. I didn't know what I was doing but trudged through until one morning I was pumping breast milk and wondered why the milk was pink. My inexperience with latching was showing. I'll spare you the gory details so let's just say that I was raw and in so much pain but could not, would not give up. I was devastated to think that I wouldn't be able to nurse her if I started giving her formula while I healed. God knows our limits and He knows our needs. A few weeks later I was ready to try again and she latched on like a pro. God is good and I felt the blessing. She nursed until she was almost nine months old.

She continued to grow and her father and I enjoyed every moment. She has always been our tender-hearted warrior, loving everyone and always willing to serve others. She truly has a beautiful heart. What a blessing she has been.

Fast forward four years later when we decided that it's time for another baby or at least time to start talking about it. I am a planner and need time to get used to changes so when we had barely started considering another child, and I suspected that I may already be pregnant, I panicked. I bought a pregnancy test in order to remove any doubt. I remember that day like it was yesterday. I waited for the results and prayed, asking God for a false alarm. I didn't feel I could love another child the way I loved my daughter. I couldn't fathom that idea. When the results were ready I was afraid to look, but mustered up the courage anyway. When I saw the blue negative sign I dropped to my knees, put my head down, and cried a deep painful cry. At that very moment I knew I was so wrong. I knew then and there that I wanted another child and that there was so much more love to be given.

This time around it was just not happening. We tried for a little over a year and nothing. I started feeling like it was my fault because I put it off for so long or because back then I wasn't sure if I wanted to do it at all. I was stressing myself out in a big way. Once I finally let go and relaxed, that's when at long last it happened. We were elated! The pregnancy this time around was almost identical. I lost another fifteen pounds before I ever gained an ounce. That quickly changed after the first six months. I enjoyed it all the same. This one was a "live one" I thought to myself. I remember being in church while they played the worship music and feeling my belly move to the beat. He's been dancing ever since. I can't seem to keep that boy still. He's a character and just the thought of him makes me smile. My gorgeous boy was born on January 22nd, 2003. Everything was great at the hospital, and luckily this time around, nursing was a cinch for a pro like me.

Once we were home something was different. I couldn't put my finger on it but it was like a dark cloud was trying to swallow me up. My four-day-old baby had to be hospitalized for severe jaundice and something inside me broke. I didn't understand it then, I felt like a bad mother. I was experiencing postpartum depression and I didn't know it. All I could do was cry and feel like I was no good for him. My poor baby was barely on this Earth for a week and I didn't think I could do right by him. It still pains me to remember. He was in the hospital alone because I wasn't allowed to stay in the NICU overnight. I was only allowed to visit for feedings and that was just a brief moment before I had to put him back in the incubator where I couldn't touch or hold him and he had to wear a mask over his eyes. I felt he needed physical touch not through rubber gloves. With his eyes covered I was consumed with irrational thoughts of him feeling abandoned. I was so distraught with the thought that I would never be able to bond with him that I spiraled downward. He was there for four days before we were finally able to bring him home. Four weeks later my baby boy seemed to develop a bit of a cold which in turn became bronchiolitis. We stood there with the ER doctors and a wave of fear hit me when they told us he would need to be admitted. Old feelings started resurfacing. He went from bad to worse very quickly. They poked and prodded to find his right lung had collapsed, therefore in need of breathing assistance. Suggestions of meningitis slowly drove me toward that dark hovering cloud. He was in that hospital for eight days. Those were the darkest days of my life. Going through that taught me to treasure him all the more. I fought that depression for him and came through.

Here we are, ten years later my kids are both strong and healthy. Now fourteen and ten years old and both are treasures that have made me richer than I could have ever dreamed. I've home schooled as well as sent them to public schools and have enjoyed them every step of the way. Through the years what I've come to discover is that no matter how hard it's been, it doesn't compare to how much fuller life is with them in it. When I look back I don't think of sleepless nights, pain, or fear. I only remember love, feeling loved by these tiny people that trust and love unconditionally. I remember finding crayon scribbled notes that said *Mommy you're the bestest*. I remember hugs, tickle time, and so much joy from these little ones. They are an inspiration to me and have made me a better person. They are my treasures, but most importantly they are my heart and I can't imagine life without them.

I recognize that everyone's situation is different but know this: life will always be so much richer with them in it.

"Every good gift and every perfect gift is from above"

– James 1:17 –

Motherhood Perfection
Thomasina Martin

Every mother, regardless of race, creed, religion, or sexual preference, falls victim to the trap known as motherhood perfection. Often this trap is set by creating a vision of what most of us think parenting should look like. This includes being a super-mom—the ill-fated attempt to become a mother who can do it all. Let's face it, the media puts pressure on us mothers to raise our children in such a way that we run ourselves ragged trying to reach a certain level of parenting perfection. We can read, plan, and even create a systematic parenting design as to how we are going to raise our children. However, time will pass, and we, as mothers, still have to journey on with our own lives.

As a single mother to a six-year-old son, I admit that I have fallen into the trap of motherhood perfection. I tried doing it all: work, school, raising my son based on my ideal parenting plan. My birth plan worked out as I had hoped, so I assumed I was doing something right. As the years passed, and my son grew, I noticed I couldn't keep up. I couldn't buy my son all the toys the other children at play dates had. I was going broke trying to buy name brand clothes. The payments on the fancy car were outrageous. I didn't own my home, and I was falling apart mentally, physically, emotionally, and financially. I wasn't reaching my goals. My parenting plan was failing.

In my mind, I had failed. I felt that I was a disappointment to my son. How could I go on knowing that the one thing I prided myself on, being the perfect parent, had gone incredibly off beam? I couldn't figure out what precisely went wrong or where I had exactly screwed up. A tremendous amount of pressure fell on me and it distracted me from being the parent I should have been from the start. I never fully comprehended that I had to continue living and face the cards that were dealt to me.

While worrying about my parenting ability, I neglected to pay attention to myself and missed that something was physically wrong with me. My body was not performing as it should have been. To make matters worse, during self-examination, I discovered a lump in my right breast. My son was almost two. Those fearsome nights before the surgery, I held my baby while crying and praying, "Oh God, have mercy on me. Please allow me the opportunity to raise my son into a wonderful God-fearing man. Let me be here for kindergarten, graduation, college, and all the other great experiences of his life." Needless to say, depression had taken over. Rather, fear of the unknown had taken over.

The day of the surgery I hugged and kissed my boy like never before. I couldn't let him go. I framed his beautiful smile in my mind; similar to the way a camera captures memories. I needed to promise him that I was going to get better. I was not willing to give up. I had him to fight for. I had to survive. This was my first encounter of true motherhood perfection: bravery.

This was a characteristic I was somehow able to add to my individuality. I wanted my son to be brave in difficult situations, but I had never before discovered that I had to lead by example. I was going to overcome this battle no matter what it took. By the grace of God, I came out of surgery with my right breast still intact and with the news that I was cancer free! The lump was benign. My son still had his mother, and I developed a will for us to live the best lives we could. However, I began feeling like a failure as a parent again.

Shortly after healing physically and mentally from the benign lump, I still felt my body was losing functionality. I was twenty-seven-years-old with no energy and no strength. I didn't sleep. I began experiencing a deep depression and feelings of anxiety. I ached and became accustomed to pain. After being evaluated by numerous doctors, I was diagnosed with severe fibromyalgia; a chronic disorder that resulted in stiff muscles, lack of strength and ability, deprived sleep, anxiety and depression, and brain haziness. I thought, "Oh how wonderful is this! Let's place one more check-mark in the failing parent category."

Not only did the diagnosis affect me, but it affected my ability to parent. It became difficult to play with my son on the floor. I didn't have the energy to wheel around trains from room to room. My parents had to step in for walks and trips to the park. Lifting my son into my arms hurt. My speech was affected by the brain haze, so remembering simple words such as spoon was at times challenging. Naturally this increased the feelings of anxiety and depression. I was frustrated by this disruption to our lives. I wanted to feel normal again. I wanted my son to have a normal mother.

As the years passed and my son grew older, I continued feeling like a failure. I kept comparing myself to everyone else. This included those around me, the moms on television, and the perfect mothers I read about in books and magazines. What type of mother had I become? I couldn't keep up with the housework, I had to quit working. I had to give up the fancy car because I couldn't afford the payments anymore. I needed continual care and support from my family and friends. Although I had support, depression and anxiety continued to grow because no matter what I did, I couldn't reach my idea of motherhood perfection. This unrealistic pressure I placed on myself transpired around the same time I mysteriously developed non-epileptic seizures.

Those around me were normal. I watched them working, cleaning, attending play dates, cooking, dating, and taking vacations all while raising children. Why couldn't I have just one piece of their world? I continually cried out to God through prayer and Biblical study begging for an answer as to what I had done to deserve each punch that came my way. I didn't get a spiritual answer right away, but then it came to me. I finally realized that it was my idea of motherhood perfection that was ultimately destroying me.

Although it is important to have goals and to continually grow as an individual and as a mother, I learned that I had to make sure my goals were attainable. Finally, at the age of thirty-one, I have gotten a clear understanding of my very own motherhood perfection. I learned it does not exist. It is unattainable. Reaching for it will suck the very breath out of my body. I've learned that if I do not take care of myself, I cannot take care of my wonderful, amazing son.

I've learned to take on the unforeseen complications in life. This means there are days when the house does not get cleaned, or toys and laundry don't get put away. I value time with my son as more important than materialistic items that eventually get used and reduced in value. I now love myself and my life just the way it is. When I need to escape, I do so by practicing yoga and meditation. I pray more and love harder. The best lesson learned is that I can only be me. What works for me and my son, may not work for anyone else. Every mother has to determine what works best for her and her family. Putting these discoveries into practice is how I've managed to reach, and live, my idea of motherhood perfection. It is my hope that every mother can do the same.

Three Times a Miracle
Donna Reedy
co-written by Jillian Amodio

Motherhood is an amazing gift. It is a gift that many people seem to take for granted. Babies are born every day but for some of us, it's just not that easy. I have always wanted to be a mom. I wanted to experience the joy of bringing a new life into the world. I wanted the responsibility of raising that tiny life, and I wanted the privilege of watching that baby grow into the wonderful person they were destined to become.

Pregnancy is the most natural thing in the world. It is the very thing that keeps humanity alive. New lives are created each and every day. These new lives shape the future of the world we live in. Pregnancy and motherhood come so easy to some. But for others, well, we just have to fight a little harder to earn the title of mother.

I, along with thousands of other women, suffered from endometriosis. This was only the beginning of my fertility struggles. After trying to conceive naturally for quite some time and failing time and time again, it became clear that something was not right. I began to fear that my dream of motherhood was ending before it had even begun. I was willing to do just about anything to make this dream come true.

In 1989, I sought out the medical advice and expertise of a team of fertility doctors at John's Hopkins. They were running a series of clinical trials regarding fertility issues at the time. It was a very selective project and I prayed night and day that I would get in. I endured painful hormone shots daily and spent more time in doctor's offices and waiting rooms than I ever thought possible. Each time I sat in a room full of other couples hoping for the miracle of conception, I silently prayed that my hormone levels would remain high enough to keep me in the trials. Whenever someone was dropped from the trials I felt even more grateful that I was still being given the chance at motherhood, something I wanted so desperately.

After months of uncertainty, I finally found out that I was pregnant. I was overwhelmed with feelings of joy, excitement, and even disbelief. I had never been happier in my life.

The joy I felt upon first finding out that I was pregnant only grew as time went on. In fact it grew three times as much as I learned that I was not carrying one precious life, but three. I was eight weeks pregnant when I found out I was carrying triplets. The nurse and the doctor were nearly as excited as I was. This was just as much their success as it was mine. My triplets would be the first set of triplets born through the John's Hopkins In Vitro Fertilization program. Watching three tiny hearts beating at my first sonogram was the most amazing, breathtaking, miraculous thing I had ever seen. I was ecstatic. Immediately after the visit I went to the pay phone (it was the dark ages back then) and I called my husband and my mom. My mom was overjoyed. My husband was...well silent. When the initial shock wore off he was just as excited as I was.

Throughout the pregnancy, I was very worried about the tiny lives growing inside of me. The pregnancy was very high risk and I lived in constant worry that something was going to happen to my precious babies. When I was four months pregnant, I began to experience complications and I feared that we were in serious trouble. When I called the doctors, they said that there was nothing we could do but wait and see. I had to be very careful; I could not lift over ten pounds and had to be cautious throughout my entire pregnancy. I quit bowling and other strenuous activities. I went on bed rest at nineteen weeks. My babies were so tiny and my stomach was so big that throughout the duration of my pregnancy, I only felt them move one time.

On a Friday I went to visit the NICU where my babies would surely end up. I went back for my regular appointment the following Monday and was not feeling very well; I was shocked when the doctors told me that I was already at four centimeters. At only thirty weeks, my babies were born via C-section at 3:48 p.m. I didn't even get to see my precious angels until 10:00 that night. I was overjoyed that I was finally a mother to three miracle babies, but nothing could prepare me for the heartache I would experience at seeing those three tiny lives hooked to respirators, confined to incubators in the NICU. Each one of my triplets weighed just over two pounds. Together they were the size of one average baby.

Three days after my sweet babies were born I stood in the NICU staring at their tiny bodies hooked up to countless machines, oxygen, and IVs, and silently wondered *My God what have I done to these poor babies?* My heart was breaking for them. I cried inconsolably.

We were the lucky ones. My three babies, although very premature, were relatively healthy. Other families were not nearly as fortunate. There was another baby right next to mine who needed a heart transplant. I remember praying that he would get the transplant he needed but that it would not be one of my babies that had to die for him to get it. He did end up getting the transplant and I stayed in contact with his family for a short time, but sadly he did not make it past eighteen months due to complications.

There was another set of twins who were born with their intestines on the outside of their bodies. One lived and one did not. There were so many sick babies in there and it was more than anyone's heart could take. We all cried together, hoped together, prayed together, and celebrated whatever small milestones we could achieve.

My heart broke for the parents who would not be able to take their angels home, but I rejoiced as my babies continued to grow more every day.

We visited them daily and longed for the day they would come home. It was hard to watch as each day my babies were fed through a tube. I remember one day I came in and they had moved them to another spot in the NICU. My heart dropped and I was nearly sick to my stomach when I walked in and did not see them. I thought I had lost my babies; I completely panicked. The nurses rushed over and immediately brought me to their new spot.

One of my babies, my boy, had a heart defect but it was fortunately corrected with medicine. I swear, looking back I wonder how I had the strength to watch all that these babies were going through, but I loved them so much that somehow I found the strength to deal with all of the hardships. I had wanted these babies so badly but I had no idea all of the trials and hardships we would have to endure after they made their entrance into this world.

The day arrived when we could take our little ones home. After over a month in the NICU, our two girls came home on Father's Day 1990, our boy came home a week later. They came home on monitors and stayed on them for eight months. We had round the clock help from family and a home nurse for the first week. Every time a monitor went off, everyone jumped up and rushed in to see what the problem was. Fortunately it was usually nothing more than a loose wire. We wouldn't even unhook the monitors for pictures. It was such a relief when the babies were doing well enough that they were no longer needed.

Having all three babies home was the best day of my life. I remember dancing around the living room holding my babies and just loving life. We were so lucky. Our babies continued to grow and thrive without any sort of birth defects or complications often associated with premature births.

My babies are now twenty-three years old and every day I look at them and cannot believe how lucky I am to be their mother. I truly do believe that they are my miracle babies. My kids are my life.

Going through fertility struggles and finally being blessed with three precious lives makes me even more aware of the fact that every life is precious. It breaks my heart when I hear of children being mistreated in any way. There are so many families who would gladly give anything and everything to bring a baby into their lives. Every baby is a miracle and every baby deserves to be loved.

"My daughter and her cousin see the same pediatrician. When we went for her eighteen-month check-up, her pediatrician said, 'Your Mimi says you like to make up songs. Can you sing one for me?' She thought about it for a second and much to my horror repeated these words to the tune of Wheels on the Bus.

'Mommy likes to drink some wine, drink some wine, drink some wine, Mommy likes to drink some wine all day long.'

Fortunately my pediatrician is a fellow wine lover and thought it was 'awesome.'

P.S. I do not drink wine all day long."

— Jillian Amodio —

Life Is Not Always Easy, But It Is Beautiful
Shirley Bailey

While in my thirties, I became ill and was hospitalized numerous times before the doctors told me I have Crohn's Disease. This was all just a few years after I settled into married life and came as a shock to me and my family. My gynecologist said I was very sick and could not get pregnant. Within one week I *was* pregnant—with twins! I had major surgery while pregnant and multiple doctors said that the babies would not survive. As sick and weak as I was, I did not believe that! I knew in my heart of hearts that the babies were a gift from God. It was a risky pregnancy, and the girls were born two months early, at roughly three pounds each. But they thrived and filled our lives with laughter and love! Two miracles!

I became a working mom and wife. My life was very full. A short time later, we had our baby boy and life was even better, if that's possible. Yearly vacations to the beach, big birthday bashes, the sweet smell of babies, and the sound of laughter filled our lives. I focused more and more on my children and less and less on my career, eventually taking lower paying jobs closer to home.

In 2009, when I was only forty-three, something very unexpected happened. My husband became ill. Within four months of being diagnosed, he died of cancer. I was suddenly a widow and a single mother. My boy was only six and the twins were just a week past their thirteenth birthday when their daddy passed away. My life was thrown into turmoil. I could not function or think clearly at work and subsequently lost my job. The part of my life I thought was most important—making money and being successful—paled to the needs of my children. I became focused on being the best mom I could, while also mourning my best friend of the past nineteen years. The words I spoke to console the kids finally soaked into my soul and gave me strength to rally us on to healing.

I had been a regular church-goer in my childhood and carried the love of God into my adult life. I taught my children to pray and took them to church. But I started to question God's will and was very angry that my prayers were not answered. I couldn't understand why God had let this happen to us. My faith faltered, and I had to rebuild the fabric of my beliefs. I spent years contemplating just about everything until I came to terms with the reality of the matter. I could mourn forever and would probably become a shell of a miserable person, or I could pick myself up and move on. Remaining as I was would not help the kids or honor my loved one's memory. I reached out to God, and He was still there for me. He understood my anger and helped me let it go. I began to have hope for the future.

I prayed for peace of soul over the loss of my husband, who was only thirty-nine. I prayed for patience and love in my relations with the children. I was granted these wishes. I prayed for another man who I could love and who would take away some of the terrible emptiness I was feeling. I was granted this wish as well and have a man in my life who is my best friend and treats me like a princess.

I slowly gained confidence and began to look for a job. I had a few interviews before it became clear to me that I was sick again, but this time it was not Crohn's, but another autoimmune disorder—multiple sclerosis. My disease is severe to the point that I cannot walk well, use my hands, or think clearly. I spend most days in bed so I have a lot of time to contemplate all that has happened and what it all means. I do not question fate or God's will, but know that I am here for a purpose. I can't have all my prayers answered, but God takes care of me. My biggest joys are my children because in them I still have a huge piece of my late husband right here on Earth. In loving them, and myself, I honor God, and that is something I can live with.

A Deeper Love
Beck Gambill

The moment is etched into my memory. The moment I realized I had given birth to my own motherhood at the same time I had birthed my precious son. The wonder of it took my breath away and the echo of my own mother's words "You'll understand when you are a mother," floated back to me over the waves of time.

I was alone in a cozy hospital room on a Sunday. My husband was at church and the visitors had abated for a few hours. Honestly it was a relief to have some quiet time to study my tiny boy. It's amazing the power of certain moments, even after years the edges haven't dulled, the details stand out as strong as ever. I remember the smell of his breath, the curve of his pink cheek traced by my finger in delight, the sighs of his contented sleep.

I was certain my heart would burst from the sheer magic of it all. I couldn't be more proud of that precious baby, my precious baby! Propped up in the hospital bed by an army of pillows, soaking in the beauty of the morning with my newborn tucked securely in the crook of my arm, I remember the amazing realization striking a clear note. The power of my love for this helpless tiny human astonished me, and the subsequent realization that this was just a shadow of God's perfect love, set my head spinning.

Tears streamed down my cheeks as I realized for the first time the parental love my heavenly Father has had for me all along. Only now was the window open. I could never understand the completeness of God's love until I held my own child in my hands. Until I risked rejection by a child, felt the pang of concern for his safety and well-being, until I delighted in my son's presence and celebrated him just being him. I had known God's love, but I hadn't grasped it as clearly as this.

What could this little human offer? Nothing. He couldn't speak my language, contribute to our household income, shoulder any responsibility, create a work of art, or enhance our quality of life. Quite the contrary, he would deprive me of sleep for months, make messes he would never help clean, increase the noise of our home as well as our responsibility, be unable to communicate, and challenge our parental resources. Oddly enough none of those realities defined my love for him, if anything his helplessness endeared him to me more.

And so it is with God. I have had to learn his language, I make messes he has to clean up, I pitch fits and cry about what I dislike, in every way I am not his equal. And yet God's love for me is defined by his own nature and is a response to my need. While I was expecting my baby, I had assumed the child was the gift, but I had been wrong. God always gives us the gift of Himself and in the package of my child He had revealed the depths of His love.

I love my son, I've grown with him and been amazed by him. But I've realized he himself is not the gift. The longer I'm a mother, the more convinced I am that the greatest blessing is a deeper need for God's love and a deeper understanding of God's love for me.

"My daughter loves animals. One day she sadly announced that she wanted to be a veterinarian when she grew up but could never do it. You see, she also loves to *eat* animals and she thought veterinarians had to be vegetarians by law!"

— Rachael Moshman —

Motherhood Made Me Who I Am

Carin Clark

What am I going to tell my mom? How do I explain this to my family and friends? I don't want anyone to be disappointed in me. These thoughts flew through my mind as I read the results of the pregnancy test. At the age of sixteen, I tested positive for B-A-B-Y. Becoming a mother at such a young age had an almost indescribable impact on my life. It is hard to put into words what it means to have your entire life shaped by one event, before you can truly grasp the gravity of it all. In the blink of an eye I went from being a kid to a responsible adult. Ready or not, here he came. The birth of my oldest son was the single most important thing that has ever happened to me. Everything that I am, everything that became of my life, stemmed from my being a mom.

As I've gotten older, I find myself seeking other moms to mingle with. Now the mother of three, I often have some sort of crazy tale to share. And I love hearing all the stories that other moms tell because it makes me feel less alone. Somehow, if I am not the only one then it must all be okay. This is totally normal if everyone else goes through it too, right? Oh, the things we tell ourselves to justify the craziness that is motherhood. What I notice in many of the conversations I have with other moms, most of who became mothers at a later age, is how much they talk about their lives before children; or how their children have made such an impact on them that they cannot imagine their lives without their children. What is always hanging in the back of my mind is how opposite my journey has been; how I can totally envision a life without my children. The path of a young mom, versus one that becomes a mother at a later age, is very different. I am sure every mother-to-be has the same fear of whether they will get it right or screw up another human being completely. But when you are young, you are still growing up. You are still learning who you are. You are still figuring out what you mean to the world. Motherhood is no different. It changes you and continues to define you.

At thirty-four-years-old I have lived more than half of my life as a mom. As a kid you aren't paying attention. You aren't making life decisions. You aren't responsible for anyone; not even yourself. For me, all of that changed the day I found out I was pregnant with my son. I had no clue what I was going to do with my life or what I was going to be when I grew up— suddenly, none of that mattered. God delivered the importance of my life on Wednesday July 23, 1997 at 3:34 p.m. And while I truly do love all three of my children more than anything else in this world, I would be lying if I said I don't often fantasize about what it would be like to have a life of my own. I don't know what that's like, so of course I wonder. There is a part of me that always will. My children are my life. Literally. Every single thing I do is fueled by my desire for my children—either to escape their grasp for a few hours, to provide them with a new experience, or to share in our fond memories. And every motivation that exists within me is attributable to my drive to create a better life for my children while also showing them how to build their own bright futures. My career, my home, my business, and my passion have all been a product of motherhood. Who I am as an adult, who I am as a person, is all connected to that single most important fact of my life: I am a mom.

I sometimes imagine that becoming a mom at a later age could have been so much fun. I would have gone to college right after high school. Earned a graduate degree soon after and then started my career. My husband and I would have dated throughout college, gotten married in a lavish ceremony after graduation, and we would have worked our way to the tops of our fields. The majority of our early years would have been spent traveling the world—Paris, Italy, Dubai, South America—and checking off the experiences on our bucket lists (skydiving anyone?). Once we had thoroughly lived every inch of our late twenties to early thirties, we would have considered slowing down and having a family. At that point, my children would have become an extension of my well-lived life. They would become a new perspective, a different motivator, and a joyous way to see life from another angle.

My life as a young mother is the total opposite of what I described above. Once I had my first child, I ceased to be an individual. I had started a family. I was faced with the monumental responsibility of having to take care of this other little person. I have traveled plenty, and spent lots of fun nights out with the girls, but it's never without preparation. Who is going to watch the kids; what time do I have to drop them off; when I am going to pick them up; and lots of "how are the kids doing?" calls in-between. I don't have a life that doesn't include my children; and as an adult, I never have. They are the core of my being—I don't know any other way to exist.

Everything I am, and everything I have, is because I am a mom. Motherhood is my core. It has been the driving force behind my career choices, my determination to get a higher education, and my passion for supporting parents and families. Motherhood revealed my path. Motherhood paved the way. Motherhood made me who I am.

"I was extremely tired from working overnight. I made myself stay awake until it was nap-time for my little Destinee Marie. Well, somebody faked their sleep until I went to sleep. She got ahold of some permanent markers from my office area and decided to give herself a make-over. Not only was I completely surprised, she looked flawless."

— Lakita Thompson —

Ready or Not
Michelle Love

Jon and I had talked many times about when we should start adding to our family. I am seven years younger than my husband, and being the one who carries the baby, I never felt the need to rush the process due to age. Jon has always said that he didn't want to be an old dad. He wanted to be able to play ball with his kids, see them graduate, and watch them grow without his older age interfering. He has always wanted to be a hands on kind of dad.

I remember talking with him in the kitchen one afternoon about whether or not we should try to get pregnant before he was to deploy to Iraq for a year. We were patient with each other and allowed each other to voice our opinions on whether or not we should try for a baby. My husband absolutely adores children. He always jokes with me that he wants to have twelve kids. Yeah ok…

He expressed how he wanted to get the process started and at least try for a baby before he left. I, on the other hand, was thinking he was insane to even be suggesting this. I said, "No way! What woman on Earth would want to get pregnant right before her husband deploys for a year? Definitely not this one!" After speaking for a while, we finally decided that we would wait. Jon was very understanding and finally came to see my point of view that this situation would be less than ideal…for me especially.

We went on with our lives and started to prepare for the deployment. We owned a home that the two of us lived in along with our two dogs. I had a great job at the time and planned on working full time while he was gone. I knew it was going to be hard but I also knew I would be able to get through. My family lived about sixty-five miles south of me, so if I ever needed anything I could count on them. I also had so many close friends and neighbors that would be there for me.

The weeks continued to pass. There was so much anxiety and anticipation in those few weeks before the servicemen actually left. It was a Sunday evening, I was visiting a friend and she randomly asked me, "Are you sure you're not pregnant?" At first it was a definite "Yes, I'm sure I'm not pregnant!" then as I sat there and thought, *Actually, I'm not really sure?*

I went home that night and took a pregnancy test; it was positive. I was shocked. I was upset. I called my husband who was in training that day and told him the news. He was extremely understanding toward me and was supportive.

I found out I was pregnant with our first child two weeks to the day, before my husband was going to be leaving. I was devastated. I called my mom crying. I remember going to dinner with my family and sobbing because I didn't want to be pregnant at that time. Why now when my husband was leaving and would have to miss everything about our first pregnancy? I was so distraught and I felt this way for at least several weeks. I just didn't want to be pregnant.

After my first doctor's appointment, I started to feel more excited about being pregnant. At my appointment I was able to see the tiny little bean growing inside of me. It was amazing to hear the heartbeat for the first time. That moment changed everything for me. I heard the heartbeat of a tiny human being that was alive inside of me and developing all her tiny features at that very moment. That was a turning point for me. I was actually happy.

I had several family members with me on the day we found out the gender, and we were able to Skype so my husband could find out at the exact same time. On that day, we were told we would be having a little girl!

Although my pregnancy was easy and quite pleasant physically, I still didn't have my husband by my side. At times it was very lonely. I continued working at my job until October of 2010 when I decided I was too lonely living by myself and needed to move in with my family. I needed to be around people for support and I had also made the decision that I would continue to live with them after the baby was born, until my husband was to return in May 2011. I would need the help after the baby arrived, and I feared that I couldn't take care of her all on my own. Moving in with my family was the best decision.

My due date was February 10th. My doctor scheduled me to be induced on that day. Jon and I had talked for months about when he should take his two weeks R&R because we wanted to insure he would be here for the birth. My biggest fear throughout all of this was that my husband would miss her birth. I told my doctor at *every* one of my appointments how it was okay if the baby decided to come early, but it *had* to be after my husband got here. I told family and friends how I would *die* if I had to give birth without my husband by my side.

Jon left Iraq on January 31st, planning to be here on February 2nd and spend a week with just me and then a week with the baby and I. I had it all planned out. I envisioned everything in my head over and over. I envisioned my husband and me walking into the hospital hand in hand and having him there with me every step of the way. I pictured spending a week with him before the baby arrived and looked forward to being able to have dinner together, talk, and hold hands. I hadn't seen him in over seven months. He had never seen me pregnant (other than before he left when I was about eight weeks pregnant). He had only seen pictures of my big pregnant belly. He hadn't ever felt the baby kick or felt her hiccups. But he would be able to when he arrived.

On February 1st, I went to my last appointment before I was to be induced. I was busy that day and ran up to my appointment alone, nothing packed and wearing ball cap and sweats. My plan was to go to my appointment, then come home and get ready to pick Jon up the very next day. I was so excited to pick him up from the airport.

I got to my appointment. My doctor did the standard procedure and went ahead and checked me for dilation. He said everything was okay and left the room. As I stood up off the table, I immediately felt water dripping down my leg. My first thought was my water broke but it wasn't the gush of water I had expected. I continued to get dressed, and as I was leaving I mentioned this to one of the nurses. She suggested I hang out for thirty minutes or so and see if water continued to leak. Luckily, Jon's cousin lived nearby. I called her and asked if I could hang out there for a bit. By the time I got to my car from the office however, my pants were soaked. I knew it was my water, and I knew that my doctor had accidentally broken my water while he was checking me for dilation. My heart dropped.

Here again, just like when I found out I was pregnant, I was living my nightmare. I was alone. My worst fears had once again come to be. When the water breaks, there's no putting it off for another day or trying to wait. I knew that I would be having this baby, and it would be without my husband by my side.

Jon's cousin Kristie came with me to the hospital. Unfortunately, Kristie wasn't able to come back into the delivery room because she had her toddler. I was all alone, and I still could not believe this was happening to me. Why? Why couldn't my husband at least be there for the birth because he had missed everything else? I tried my hardest to stay composed; however I did break down from time to time because I couldn't understand why everything was happening this way.

After some time, my family was able to make it to the hospital. They all stayed in my room and tried to lighten my spirit. Jon called me while I was in labor, and I was able to talk to him. He was just about to board a plane from Germany and asked if there was any way they could hold off the delivery until he arrived. I smiled. That was the last I spoke to him until after I had Scarlett.

My delivery was very easy. Three pushes was all it took. The doctor asked me if I wanted to cut the umbilical cord and I said, "Yes! How many women get to say they did this?" I felt so proud of myself. Finally, I got to see my baby. Of course, there are no words to describe that moment. I had tears of joy running down my face. It was the happiest moment of my life.

Scarlett Love was born on February 2nd at 1:49 a.m. She weighed five pounds and eleven ounces and was eighteen inches tall. She had strawberry-blonde hair and big blue eyes, just like her daddy. I will never forget the most adorable little squeak she made. Her first noise.

The next morning Jon called me from Georgia. The first words he said were "Did you bring a baby into this world?" I teared up and said, "Yes" with a smile. At 10 p.m., Jon made it to the hospital. I was so happy and relieved to see him. It was such a proud moment for me to show him our baby girl. She was perfect.

We were able to spend sixteen days together as a little family before Jon had to go back to Iraq for another three months. It was hard to say goodbye, but I knew I would be preoccupied taking care of this new angel. Our reunion would be that much sweeter and I would have our little girl with me to greet him when he arrived home.

I learned so many things about myself during this entire experience. It wasn't ideal timing. None of it was. But because I had so much support from family and friends throughout my pregnancy, not to mention so many fun baby projects to keep me busy, I now look back and realize that my pregnancy *is* what got me through Jon's deployment. I don't do well with deployments, and had I not been pregnant I would have spent the entire eleven months sitting around moping because my husband was gone. I would have decided to spend my time focusing on being miserable. But instead, I was blessed with my pregnancy to get me through. I know this. I now know I need to trust God because He knows what's best for us, even if we don't believe it's what's best at the time.

I used to tell people I would die if Jon missed Scarlett's birth. I truly thought I wouldn't make it without him. But I am proud to say that I did. It wasn't easy, but it has made me a stronger person today. Anytime I have weak moments when I don't think I can handle something, I step back and remind myself of what I went through. I stand here a stronger person today. I feel so proud when I get to tell people that I got to cut the umbilical cord; to me it was a big deal. It showed my strength when I was going through one of my biggest nightmares.

Today I am reminded every day of how blessed I am. My two-year-old, blonde-haired, blue-eyed beauty is here as a constant reminder, and soon she will be a big sister! I now know that I wouldn't trade her for the world and I would go through it all again just to have her. It was all worth it. All of it. All of the struggles, tears, heartbreaks, fears, along with all of the joy. I will never regret having her and am so glad that God knew me well enough to give me a situation, though not ideal, that I needed.

"My two-year-old daughter repeats everything...

She and Daddy were playing with her princess figurines. Daddy picked up Belle (who's make-up is a little smudged) and said, 'Juliette, is Belle pretty?'

Juliette said, 'She's a hot mess!'"

— Jillian Amodio —

Becoming Mommy
Amy Orzechowski

Being a mommy is not something I dreamed about as a child. I am a very career-driven woman, and I saw my life revolving around my work. In my mid-twenties I was married and still serving on active duty in the U.S. Army. Then I found out I was pregnant. It was the happiest day of my life. I was elated to know that I would soon be a mom. While I was scared of what having a baby would mean for my military career, I couldn't wait to meet the tiny one growing inside of me. I couldn't wait to find out the gender of my little being, so as soon as possible I learned that we were having a girl.

My pregnancy was going pretty well until at thirty-four weeks I was diagnosed with severe preeclampsia and had to be induced. I waited on bed rest in the hospital until my body decided that it couldn't wait anymore. This was undoubtedly the most difficult time in my life. I selflessly feared for the health and life of my unborn daughter. I had already grown to love her so much, and I could not face the thought of her being in danger.

On August 11, 2005 I became Mommy to a precious girl. She changed me completely. My work was no longer my top priority, the happiness and well-being of my baby was. I cut my military career short to ensure that I was home to spend every day possible with my baby.

A few years later, I divorced and my angel was now my sole responsibility. My life revolved around her, and it still does to this day. Every decision I made whether it was regarding my career, the choices in food that I made at the grocery store, or where to live—each and every decision was made with her best interests in mind. A few years ago I remarried and again did not expect to have any more children. After such a rough pregnancy and childbirth with my first daughter, I thought that attempting another pregnancy would be dangerous.

My new husband and I deliberated a while over having another child. Deep down we both wanted to have a baby together. After thinking it over for quite some time, we decided we were going to go for it. Miraculously, a few weeks later I was pregnant! We were both so elated at the thought of growing our family. I couldn't wait for my baby to have a sibling. Of course what I wanted most was to have a healthy baby, but if I could ask for one more favor, it was to have a second healthy little girl.

Again, as soon as possible, we found out the gender and were thrilled to find out that we were having a girl! My second pregnancy was much like the first; it was fairly easy except for the horrible heart burn. At twenty-eight weeks however, things started to go downhill and again I was diagnosed with preeclampsia. This time I was given some blood pressure medication and put on best rest at home. I went for bi-weekly check-ups and my health continued to decline. At thirty-four weeks the doctors decided it was time to induce and deliver the baby. I was so scared that something was going to happen to my baby. My husband was even more scared than me. Not only was he worried about his baby girl, but he was worried about his wife as well.

On March 23, 2012 my second little angel was born healthy.

I could not be more blessed. I have two precious daughters both extremely healthy and thriving. While being a mommy was not something I dreamed of, motherhood is a blessing that I could not live without. My babies are my world. I am still very dedicated to my full-time career but I am equally dedicated to my life as a mommy. My babies light up my evening when I get home. My heart fills with joy to see their smiles and hear their laughter! I would not give up motherhood for anything.

The Ups and Downs of Single Parenting

Kaytlin Brown
co-written by Jillian Amodio

My life as a mother can best be compared to a roller coaster ride. It has been full of ups and downs, twists and turns, thrills, fear, excitement, and uncertainty. But I suppose life tends to be like that—unpredictable.

My journey started when I found myself to be pregnant. I had not planned on becoming a mother so young. I had not planned on being a single parent. I was surprised, I was shocked, and I was scared. But overwhelmingly, I was excited. There is no feeling that can compare to the moment you find out you are going to become a mom. Suddenly you realize that you are not living life for yourself anymore.

On December 8, 2009 my life changed in ways I never imagined possible. After nine long months and four full days of labor, I welcomed my darling baby girl into my life. As I gazed into the eyes of my newborn daughter I realized that there was nothing more rewarding than being a mom. All of the hardships, fear, and uncertainty faded away as I looked into the eyes of the child I had created.

I can't explain why, I can't explain how; all I know is that in that precious fleeting moment of my daughter's birth, I felt complete. I became whole. I knew I had to do this on my own, I knew that the life of a single mom was bound to be difficult, but I also knew that no matter what life had in store for us, we would make it through just fine.

When my daughter was nine months old, her father decided that he was ready to step up to his role in our lives. He wanted to try to be a father to his daughter, and a partner to me. I was excited to finally be a family. I had never wanted to be a single mother at the age of twenty. I had dreams, goals, and aspirations. I had a plan. I had wanted to go to school and become a nurse. I wanted a picture perfect family and to live a comfortable, happy life surrounded by those I loved. With my baby's father back in the picture, it felt like those dreams might finally be obtainable.

I put everything I had into making our life together perfect. I wanted so badly for things to fall into place and stay that way. I found out the hard way that you just can't force something that isn't meant to be.

I found myself to be pregnant again; this time with a little boy. This pregnancy was not exactly planned either, but children are a gift no matter how or when they come into this world. Sadly the pressure of the whole situation proved to be too much for the father of my children. He left us and I was once again alone. Now, not only was I facing the prospect of raising one child on my own, but two.

I knew it was going to be a challenge, but with faith and family I knew I would persevere and come out stronger in the end. On June 11, 2011 I welcomed my second child into the world—a beautiful baby boy. Once again my world had been flooded with more happiness, love, and laughter than I had ever known.

Three days later, that happiness was shattered. My son was showing signs that something might be wrong. At eight weeks old, my son weighed only an ounce more than he had at birth. He was referred to a GI specialist at Children's Hospital. The doctor made the difficult decision to admit him to the hospital in an effort to get his weight on track. My heart was broken. I cannot explain the depth of the pain a mother feels when she looks into the face of her suffering child. This was only the beginning of an uphill battle to determine the cause of my son's symptoms.

My son has seen countless doctors and has undergone a multitude of surgeries. Over a year later, we still do not have a solid answer as to what is causing my son's ill health, all we know is that the doctors are doing the best they can and we need to keep our hopes up and stay strong in our faith. It would be all too easy to give up, to throw my hands in the air and say, "What more can I do?" As a mother, giving up is not an option. The only thing to do is move forward and love your children. My children are my source of strength. They are the reason I wake each day.

My journey through motherhood has been a crazy one. It has had its moments of despair and heartache, but no matter how difficult things get, I will never regret the decisions I have made. I love being a mother. It truly is the most rewarding thing I have ever done. There is no love like the love you receive from a child.

My story has not been all heartache. I finally met a man I could trust; a man I love, but more importantly, a man who loves me and my children. He has given my children the father they deserve and has restored my belief that true love exists. He has been with us through surgeries, doctor's appointments, tears, and laughter. He has been with us through the good times and the bad.

No matter when we become a mother and no matter how. No matter if it was planned or unplanned, wanted or not, we all go through times of hardship. The road to (and through) motherhood is full of bumps and detours. We all feel like giving up at some point. What keeps us going is the smiling faces of our children and the knowledge that their happiness is the most important thing in the world.

No matter how tough things get, your children will always be the light at the end of the tunnel, letting you know that all will be okay. You are not alone. You will never be alone. You can, and will always have the strength to fight for the happiness that you deserve.

My Love Is Like a Sunset
Kristi Dalnoky

Not too long ago I was thinking about my postpartum experiences (I have delivered three babies to date). I began considering all of the emotions that follow a birth. You'll read about baby blues, postpartum depression, crying at the drop of a hat... Delivering a baby, combined with all of the raw and new emotions, hormone adjustments, parental responsibilities, and paradigm shifts can really create a complex experience for most, if not all, new mothers. I often think in pictures, so imagine, if you will, a work of art. Some of the brushstrokes are deliberate, detailed, prepared for, yet others are spontaneous splatters that you create in the moment and embrace with faith and abandon. That's motherhood. It's a living work of art and your life's masterpiece.

As I was considering all of this, I was struggling with the differences that came with each birth experience and the bonds I had made, or not made, with each child. When my first daughter was born, I felt such a sense of awe. She amazed me. Becoming a parent amazed me. Every moment, milestone, and detail was like a revelation. I was overcome with the desire to love and protect this child with every ounce of my being. It was a fierce and passionate love. I probably became the epitome of a helicopter mom.

Before conceiving my second daughter, I miscarried a child. The weight of that loss, coupled with a complicated third pregnancy, really wore on me—mind, body, and soul.

My second daughter, Isla, my "bright and shining one" in ancient Greek, really fought to be here, and even her birth was a battle for this mama. I can't tell you whether or not all of those things affected my ability to feel normal afterward, but normal I was not. I felt very disconnected, like I had to fight for her love. The emotions were not familiar to me, and I carried a great deal of guilt during those days. Even though I know I never had to, I would often find myself trying to win her smiles, laughter, and kisses. It was such a difference from my first go at being Mommy. It felt stormy and intense in a completely unique way. The passion was there, but the peace and security that I wanted desperately to feel was not. I feared that she wasn't getting what she needed from me, emotionally day in and out.

Nearly two years later, my third daughter came to be, and just like the second was different from the first, the third was an experience all of its own as well. With this child, I felt a peace. It was as if I acquired a new level of trust with myself and the world. No longer the helicopter mom that emerged with the first, and no longer the sad and striving mom that was ridden with anxiety after the second, I seemed to have found a stride and a balance. Then it happened. Even my peace made me feel guilty! What was it about this time around that made me feel this way? What was it about this child? Those were the tough questions that would plague me throughout the day. I struggled and wrestled and worried if any of this reflected my love for these children and if they could feel any of the effects.

And then it hit me.

Your love is like a sunset.

What?

Yes. My love is like a sunset.

I think perhaps God was depositing a little imagery into my worried mind. (After all, the One who created me knows that I think best in pictures.) A mother's love for her child is a sunset. Have you ever seen a sunset that you couldn't find beauty in? That you couldn't appreciate? Every sunset is a masterpiece. Every color, no matter how dark or light, adds to its splendor. One majestic sunset can't be stacked against another.

One child can't ever be more or less loved than another. That is my love for my babies. If I had to paint a sunset for each of my children, for the first, it would consist of fiery oranges and golds. For the second, it would be deep—made up of the most beautiful purples your eyes have ever seen. For the third, it would be serene and light, made up of wispy blues and pinks. That is my love for them. It is complex, but it is beautiful always. I no longer carry guilt when I look back on those days. Instead, I see in my mind's eye the masterpiece. I see the sunsets, and I feel the love depicted in every hue.

"Papi: Wow Sabrina, you're good
with your hair.
Sabrina: I've had hair since I was a baby
so I know what to do."
— @FunnyKidQuotes —

Becoming a Tummy Mommy
Rebekah Wishart

Two weeks after my eighteenth birthday, I found out that I was pregnant. I wasn't quite sure how it would all work out but deep down inside I knew it would.

My best friend, Grace, flew out from Colorado to be with me and be there (in North Carolina) for my sister's wedding. Grace and I flew back to Colorado on April 8th and on the sickening flight, I had this feeling I wasn't going to be in Colorado just for the summer.

At the end of April, Grace and I went to Idaho to visit Grace's aunt, uncle, and cousins. Auntie Joanie and I had some time to talk and she asked if I had considered adoption.

"Oh no, I could never do that!"

"Why?"

"Well, because. I would be carrying this baby for nine months and I know I couldn't let him go."

"Well just think. He could have an amazing life with a mommy and a daddy. You could go to school and so on."

On the trip home I fought back tears like never before. The thought of having to let go of this little one growing inside me, was painful.

A few days after we got back from Idaho a friend asked me to visit a church with her.

"Eric and Leslie Ludy go to the church," she informed me. After the service we were introduced to Eric. He started asking me about why I had come to Colorado. I finally told him I was currently fourteen weeks pregnant. He asked if I was going to parent or place the baby. I told him I was leaning more toward parenting.

"Bex, I want you to know that if you decide to place this child, Leslie and I would count it a great privilege to adopt your baby."

I smiled and nodded politely. *Okay, so maybe he is just being nice*, I thought.

Adoption did come up in my discussions with my support group, but I put it on the back burner.

Sandi, my Colorado mom, set up an appointment at Life Choices, the pregnancy resource center, so I could get my footing, some resources, etc. As we were leaving the center I was told I could pick a hat and a pair of booties for the baby. That was so very special! Over the course of the pregnancy the staff at the pregnancy center walked through a lot with me. The director made a habit of praying at the end of each visit; she encouraged me to seek God and ask Him for wisdom. Life Choices provided me with all the maternity clothing, resources, and encouragement I could ever ask for!

After about the third or fourth visit, I asked Denise, the director at Life Choices, to set up meetings with adoption agencies so I could find out what all adoption entailed. Some of my family and I were able to meet with Beth from Hope's Promise. As soon as I met Beth I liked her; she was professional yet very personable. She explained to us the different types of adoption: closed, semi-open, and open. I quickly said, "If I decide to do this it would have to be an open adoption. There is no way I could not know what was going on in my baby's life."

I had an ultrasound mid-June and found out I was having a little boy! I already knew that but I'm not really sure how…I just did! For the next few weeks I carried around the ultrasound pictures, making everyone look at them. I was becoming more and more attached to this little boy.

I was showing the ultrasound pictures to Eric and Leslie one night at church and I told them I had met with an adoption agency and was really leaning that direction. Eric asked what agency. "Hope's Promise out of Castle Rock," I said. I can't describe the look on Eric's face when I told him that. I will never forget it. Come to find out, they were meeting with someone from Hope's Promise that week! My heart jumped and my mind started running a million miles a minute.

A few days later I felt I really had to make a decision, and I knew what it should be. After some wrestling I said, "Yes." It wasn't an easy decision to make. My yes would be a yes with no backing out.

The more I got to know Eric and Leslie, the more I loved them and knew God had put us together for a reason. They were the best family I could choose to place my baby with. They championed me the entire way, always praying for me and encouraging me.

I had to prove to the court that I had looked at all my options and knew what I was doing when I chose to place my baby. This meant hours of pouring over resources and mapping out what our life could look like. This solidified my decision to place my son. I knew I could parent, but it would not be the life I would want for us.

On November 1st around 3:00 a.m., I woke up and my water had broken! I quickly called Eric and Leslie and said, "We're having a baby today!" Long story short, the labor didn't progress so my baby was born via C-section. The first cries brought tears to my eyes; I thought my heart was going to explode! I was trying not to cry so I could see him as the nurse held him up for me. I was able to look at him and touch his little cheek right before he was taken away to the nursery.

I convinced my nurse I could handle going down to the nursery to be with him. To finally be able to hold him in my arms and stare at him was one of the most wonderful feelings I have ever experienced.

As I was wheeled out of the hospital I tried to keep the tears from streaming down. But when it came time to say goodbye there was no stopping them. My heart has never ached more than it did during those few minutes of parting. Leslie was crying with me. Eric hugged me and made sure I knew that whenever I needed to see my baby they would make it happen. And then they went home, a family. And I went home with a teddy bear to fill my arms and a heart full of things I couldn't quite express.

Eric and Leslie and I chose open adoption because we wanted our son to know where he came from, why I placed him, and to have an opportunity to showcase how an open adoption can be handled. Some people are scared of open adoption, and understandably so. It is different and challenging. Communication is key. I know they care about me and want to protect our special relationship.

Trust is also important. I am very open with Eric and Leslie, and they are open with me. They don't think I am going to run off into the wild blue yonder with Kip because they know that when I chose them I was doing what I believed to be best for my son.

I've had people ask if I can get him back now that I am married. No! This is a legal adoption; I relinquished all rights as a parent and am just blessed with the opportunity to play a different part in Kipling's life: his tummy mommy.

Our adoption is open. And with that there is great peace and joy in knowing that my little boy is happy, healthy, and so very loved. It also hurts; every time I say hello I see there is so much I have missed about him growing. And when I say goodbye I will be missing more of his life. But I have chosen this and I have no regrets.

Not the Nanny
Gail Centeno

If someone told me I was going to become a mother to three children in just over three years, all by the age of twenty-five, I would never have believed them. Laughable, really.

Everyone has a story. The details are always different. Perhaps similarities exist, but our paths have different turns; unique circumstances that come to define us. Some choices, we have made. Others have been made for us. Many experiences have been for our benefit. Although, some may not have been…or at least don't necessarily seem that way at first.

Though your story may be different from mine, I'm a woman, like you. I have hopes and dreams, like you. I know what love is, like I hope you do. I've also been scared, like you may understand.

I'm a young mom.

I have a story.

Seventeen. That's the age I was when I met the man who became my husband. Tall-ish (he wishes he were taller), dark and handsome, he was twice my age. Literally. *It will never last*, people thought. Some said it to our faces. Most snickered behind our backs. Those who didn't know the depth of our relationship would never understand. Sometimes, though, you just know. And we did. He waited for me to finish college, which through extraordinary blessings, I was able to do early. We married when I was barely twenty.

After a short eleven months, I became pregnant with our first son. Amidst crazy circumstances and a series of unexplained negative pregnancy tests, I was in fact pregnant, but it wasn't confirmed until an ultrasound. I was an incredible fourteen and a half weeks along. Young and naïve, while I truly suspected I was pregnant all along, based on my calculations, I thought I was only about eight weeks. At the ultrasound, hoping to get the slightest glimpse of a tiny fluttering heartbeat (a miracle in itself), I instead saw my baby, kicking and moving his clearly defined arms and legs! It was surreal. The next months seemed to crawl in anticipation of his arrival. I guess he was anxious, too, because he arrived on the scene three weeks early. His delivery, easily the most exciting and nerve-wracking day of my life, was met with life-threatening complications. He was fine; it was me. My husband and family prayed, asking God to spare my life, especially for the sake of our newborn son. I am here today because in His infinite love, mercy and wisdom, God still had plans for me. I was only twenty-one.

Eleven months after that day, I became pregnant again. This time, the plans God had were certainly not my own and unthinkable in my mind. Before my first trimester had ended, so had my unborn child's life. Not understanding why I had to go through the pain of losing a baby, a baby I loved even before I held him or her, I felt peace. It's the kind of peace that passes all understanding, coming over you even when it wouldn't ordinarily make sense. My faith brought me through. I knew God had other plans for me. What I didn't know was that just eight weeks later I would become pregnant again. (I think it's safe to say I'm quite fertile.)

Nine months later, my beautiful daughter was placed in my arms for the first time. I looked at her in awe. I couldn't imagine not holding her. Her tiny little fingers: perfect. Her wispy little eyelashes: tender. Her sweet baby breath on my cheek: irreplaceable.

I now had a twenty-three-month-old and a newborn. Life was busy, full, and apparently not yet complete. When my daughter was seven months old, through circumstances that were clearly ordained from above, I became pregnant yet again. I would love to say that I was instantly overjoyed, that I was ecstatic at the thought of having another baby. After all, I loved my two children dearly. But, although a third child was in our plans at some point, the timing was much sooner than anticipated. I was completely overwhelmed. Scared. Fearful. I was only twenty-five. Even with the support of my husband, how was I going to handle three babies? I struggled as I thought about how my life would change even more.

Naturally though, it didn't take long, and my fear was replaced by excitement. Would he look like his brother? Would he have his daddy's toes? Would he be a snuggler like his sister? Would one of my children finally have my green eyes?

We met our precious, sweet boy, who actually doesn't have his daddy's toes or my green eyes, and is perfect all the same, a little ahead of schedule on a late September night. Nothing has been the same since. And I wouldn't have it any other way.

There I was. Twenty-five. Three babies in three years and three months' time. (Makes my head spin, too.) Double stroller and toddler trotting along, people thought I was the nanny. When they found out I was the mother, they asked if I *had* a nanny. No. My babies: my love and care.

Is it hard? Oh my goodness, yes!

I thought I would never get out of the diaper stage.

Now I realize the diaper stage was a piece of cake.

Nothing prepares you for motherhood. The joys, the heartaches, the everything. No one can fully describe that moment when you see your child for the first time, the tenderness of that unparalleled experience that takes your breath away. The instant you look into the eyes of a piece of you—a piece of our Creator.

Some of my most challenging moments have been because I am a mother. Code: It's not all sunshine and daisies. Children don't come with a handbook. (What a great idea that would be.) You don't get to choose all the fun, happy times without the this-is-hard and they're-driving-me-up-awall times. Yet, many of my best moments have been for the very same reason. I'm a mother. I have not one, not two, but three little parts of me on this Earth that share my heart. The completely normal frustrations and difficulties (ask any mom) are paled by the most incredibly heart-grabbing, awe-inspiring moments that can only come from being a mother. The thing you just can't imagine until it's here in front of you.

My children? I look at their faces and I see my eyes. I look in their eyes and I see my soul. I look in their soul and I see God.

I don't know why life turns out the way it does sometimes, but I've realized it's not my job to figure it out. I do know that "God causes everything to work together for the good of those who love God and are called according to his purpose for them." Romans 8:28

I also know that if I were in control, I'd absolutely make a mess of things. Certainly, I'm not a perfect mother, but the love for my children is greater than the times I've messed up. I'd like to think the hugs, kisses, bedtime stories, and favorite cookies after school make up for my hopefully only occasional inadequacies.

Someone once called me "just a mom" (before the days of my career). While rightfully insulted, as if it wasn't a respectable position on its own, I had to realize they didn't yet know what it really meant to be a mother. Motherhood doesn't have a comparison. It's actually difficult to adequately describe. Nothing compares to, replaces, or surpasses it. It stands in its own rank. And though little to nothing will challenge you more, I've never found an equal I'd care to replace it with anyway.

I'm a mother.

And my heart now beats three times as fast.

"Mothers are all slightly insane."

— J.D. Salinger —

No Regrets
Tammy Darrow

These kinds of things always happen to other girls. I found myself feeling alone and scared at seventeen...the day I found out I was that other girl. I was pregnant.

Coming from a dysfunctional family, I knew nothing about what it meant to be loved unconditionally. It always seemed like there was a price tag attached to that thing called love. Little did I know I was about to find out the price of it. I hid the fact from my parents for weeks as I waited to turn eighteen. I was scared and unsure of what they could and could not force me to do with my body...or my baby.

As my mother stood in the bathroom doorway yelling at me and asking what was wrong with me, I could do nothing but scream back, "I'm pregnant, all right?" And then, total silence. The silence was almost deafening for several minutes while I waited for her to speak. Nothing. After what seemed like an eternity she turned on her heel and left the room. The next sound I heard was her on the phone talking to my father saying, "Come home right now! *Your* daughter got herself pregnant." And then...she was gone. I'm not sure where she went or how I came to be at her best friend's house because looking back on it, it was all a blur. I do remember the call summoning me home. I was terrified. They were angry. Again.

The next few hours are foggy. I tend to block things out that were too emotionally traumatizing. There was a lot of yelling, cursing, threats, and bargaining. The boyfriend and his parents were summoned to our home.

He arrived alone. By that time I was numb. I had heard enough. I was beyond scared and starting to fight back. Not for myself but for that little life inside of me. I finally had to make a stand...for us. I think all three of them were dumbfounded when I made the bold statement that I was not going to have this abortion they spoke of. I was going to have *my* baby.

I was seventeen. I was going to be a mother. I was scared to death.

Six months later, six weeks before my due date, I gave birth to the most beautiful human being I had ever laid eyes on. I finally knew what unconditional love was. My heart was so full for him that I thought my heart would burst. He was the best thing I had ever fought for. Then and now.

Thirty years later I have no regrets. The relationship with the boy didn't last. I never have carried a child where my father didn't demand that I have an abortion. I have had my fair share of struggles; but I would do it all again just to look into that little boy's eyes for the first time. He was the person that made this mother's heart complete.

Pray for the Baby and Trust in God

CarmenAna Klosterman
co-written by Jillian Amodio

Pregnancy is scary for everyone; even those of us who are prepared for the arrival of a baby. We all go through hardships and times of trial. Bringing a new life into the world is exciting and miraculous, but it is also very new. Feeling anxious and afraid at some point is only natural.

I have seven children. I love them all dearly, and I thank God for bringing each one of them into my life. My story of motherhood is unlike any other. Each of our stories is unique in its own way. We all have something to learn and something to teach.

Like most stories, mine has a beginning. It began much like any other. When my husband and I were first married, we had planned on having two children. We were blessed with a beautiful daughter and a handsome son. We thought our family was complete.

Three years down the road we had built a large home and we found ourselves wanting to fill up the space with the love and laughter that only children can bring. Our desire to have two children blossomed into wanting a larger family. We had another baby, then another, and another. Our family grew and grew and we are now blessed with seven wonderful, amazing, gifted, children.

I knew that being a mother was my life's calling. After my third pregnancy, I quit working and stayed home to raise our beautiful children.

In 1993, I had the shock of my life. I found out that I had breast cancer. I was scared for myself, but even more so for my husband and our children.

It all started when I had noticed at a doctor's office that mammograms were being covered by insurance. I had not had one and I decided that there was no time better than the present. My mother had cysts and it seemed like a good idea to get things checked out. I needed a doctor's referral to set up an appointment. I called my OB/GYN. They laughed when I asked for a referral without making an appointment. It had been two years since I had seen them after the birth of my sixth child. I decided to make an appointment for after Easter.

My appointment was scheduled on a Tuesday. The doctor noticed a fullness in my breast and ordered a full mammogram regime. I had the mammogram done the next day. There were two lumps that appeared liquid. On Thursday I noticed another lump underneath my arm. It was about the size of a Ping Pong ball. I frantically called my doctor, and he suggested I call a surgeon. The surgeon had a cancellation that afternoon for 2:00 p.m. Things were happening so quickly. I could hardly think straight.

On my way to meet with the surgeon, I dropped my children off at a friend's house and called my husband asking him to meet me at the doctor's office.

The surgeon tried to drain the lumps but they were solid. Two were on tissue and two were on lymph nodes. He did a biopsy and personally took them to the lab to be tested. We met back with the surgeon on Friday and he gave us the news. They were cancerous. An operating room was reserved for the following Wednesday and a radical mastectomy was the recommended course of action.

I had to go in for blood work on Monday and I requested a pregnancy test. I was not late yet but I had a nagging feeling that I was pregnant again.

At my request the doctor simply said, "Okay, if it is positive, I will do a D and C since I will be in there already."

I didn't say a word. I just stared at him in disbelief. Where did this blatant disregard for human life come from? On Tuesday I received a call from my doctor letting me know that my suspicions were true. I was indeed pregnant. He advised us to go ahead with the surgery but would not perform the D and C to stay true to our wishes. We would pray for the baby and trust that all would be okay.

On Wednesday April 21, I underwent the mastectomy. When we got the pathology report, we found that seven of my ten lymph nodes were cancerous. I was given the name of an oncologist and told to schedule an appointment as soon as possible. On May 7, I met with the oncologist and was told that I was in need of a very aggressive form of chemotherapy. He looked me in the eye and told me that unless I aborted the baby he would not administer the treatment. He said he would "not want to be the one to deliver that baby." We said no. Abortion was not an option. This child deserved a chance at life just as much as I did.

My husband and I met with a priest who was into bio-ethics. He told us that although we could not go through with an abortion, we could go through with the treatment and place the life of our child in God's hands. To that he added "unless you feel called to give your life for the life of the baby."

I had so much to think about. I had a husband and six other children who were counting on me. I did not feel that I was being called to die so that my baby could live, but I also did not want to agree to treatment that could potentially harm my child. I said no to any treatment.

I felt so alone. I was scared and confused. I wanted to fight my cancer but I did not want to harm the innocent life inside of me. I was afraid that my husband would not agree with me wanting to defer treatment until the birth of our baby.

We didn't have to.

The following Sunday, we heard of another oncologist who was willing to see us and talk about other options. We met with him and he suggested waiting until the baby was three months in utero before starting chemo. He recommended having a stem cell transplant after our baby was born. He wanted to harvest my own cells and then transplant them back into me after I underwent the rest of my chemotherapy. The first oncologist had wanted to do this during my pregnancy, which is why they recommended having an abortion. Meeting with this new oncologist was a real blessing; this was a plan that we could get on board with, one that would offer treatment without compromising our beliefs or the life of our unborn child.

During my pregnancy, while we waited for the baby to be three months along, friends of ours sent us on a pilgrimage to Mexico. We had the opportunity and immense blessing of visiting the Basilica of Our Lady of Guadalupe. We prayed and asked for her intercession. We placed the life of our baby in her care. That brought us an overwhelming sense of peace. This was no longer a burden that we carried alone. God was with us. He always had been.

After we came back from our trip, there was more peace in our hearts. We began the chemo in July and had four rounds. We stopped as it got close to our daughter's due date. The pregnancy was overall very smooth. I had very few problems and was fortunate to have many friends who were constantly bringing meals and taking care of us. We even had a friend who paid for a window-washer to do my windows! We were so spoiled.

Our daughter grew and developed just fine. She was a fighter too. She was born full term, weighing eight pounds, four days before Christmas. What a beautiful gift she was to our family especially during a time of such uncertainty.

I had been a bit scared when I first went into labor, but she was born perfect (and she still is). I was able to nurse her for a few weeks, until the doctors gave me medications designed to stimulate cell growth to prepare my body for the stem-cell transplant.

I remember getting very sick in the hospital during the transplant. I specifically recall one of the technicians getting very close to me and telling me that I had to fight for my life. At the time, I had no clue what she was talking about.

I never felt like I was going to die, but I knew that if I did, it would be okay if that was God's will. It would have been harder for my husband and children who would be left behind.

To tell you the truth, I felt like I was being carried all along. There were so many people praying for me that I never felt anxious. I did not like losing my hair, or living in the hospital for three weeks without my children and husband. I did not like feeling sick to my stomach and losing my taste buds…and my mind. But I knew it was all temporary, and I knew that I was going to be okay.

Last year I had breast cancer again—a different kind. I went through chemo again. I lost my hair. I got sick. I got better! I beat cancer again. I was surprisingly calm with my second diagnosis. I had beat it once and I could do it again. Of course I was not doing it alone. I had the support of my family and friends, and of course I had God on my side.

My seventh baby, my miracle child, my survivor, my fighter, is now nineteen years old and in college. All of my children bring me such joy and make me so proud to be their mother.

If we had listened to the advice of doctors telling us to abort the baby, my wonderfully talented daughter would not be here. With faith, hope, and love, we both survived and are stronger because of the hardships we worked through.

Faith truly can move mountains. It can overcome all odds. Never underestimate the power of faith, hope, and love.

"Sometimes when you pick up your child you can feel the map of your own bones beneath your hands, or smell the scent of your skin in the nape of his neck. This is the most extraordinary thing about motherhood—finding a piece of yourself separate and apart that all the same you could not live without."

— Jodi Picoult (Perfect Match), author —

Lessons from my Daughter: Cherished Moments

Raquel Kato

It's amazing how much a ten-month-old can teach you about life.

I usually measure my days in terms of productivity and completed tasks. I'm a to-do list kind of girl and I thrive off of deadlines, projects, goals, and being busy.

But today was possibly one of the best days of my life.

I didn't get anything done.

Not a single task that I wanted to complete was checked off.

Today, my little girl stole my heart (for the millionth time).

Her laughter, smiles, and pure cuteness made me forget about everything I needed to get done. In fact, she made me realize how trivial those tasks really are. I put too much weight on being productive and efficient and I forget how to just be.

Being present.

That's what my daughter taught me today.

And it was one of the best days of my life. There was pure joy and freedom. Nothing was burdensome about just playing with my daughter.

As simple as it was, it was perfect.

Then, after all the playing and laughing was done and it was time for bed, she taught me yet another lesson.

As I rocked her to sleep and put her in her crib, she kept waking up and fussing. She would look at me with her big, beautiful eyes and spread her arms open to me, waiting for me to pick her up.

This happened a few times and I began to get a little irritated, thinking *AvaMarie, we had a great day, and now it's time for bed, why won't you go to sleep?*

It took me an extra half hour of rocking her to get her to sleep. But in the half hour, AvaMarie stole my heart again. My irritation quickly changed to hundreds of emotions of love, joy, and sadness.

Love and joy because I don't think there is anything closer to heaven than having a baby fall asleep in your arms. Sadness because I realized that my little baby is growing up every day. Today she didn't want me to leave her in her crib. She wanted me. She begged for me to hold her with her wide open arms. The day is quickly approaching when she won't want me to tuck her in. She won't need me to rock her to sleep. And on that day I'm going to wish with all my heart that I had cherished these moments a little more.

So today, and hopefully tomorrow, and the next day, I won't count the minutes it takes to rock her to sleep. I won't be upset when my task list goes a few extra days uncompleted. I won't take this time for granted because I can already feel it slipping away.

Thank you AvaMarie. For giving me glimpses of heaven and filling my life with joy. Thank you for reminding me that life is not about being efficient and productive but about enjoying the people you love. I love you and I will always cherish these moments.

Mothering Their Legacies
Hannah Rose Allen

Ever since I was a little girl, I always knew I was meant to be a mother. The desire was embedded deep within my heart. As a child, I literally remember having dreams about finding abandoned babies in random places such as grocery stores and me rescuing them and taking them home to forever love and care for.

I knew that being a mother was part of the calling God had for me, though I never could have imagined just how it would unfold. That one day I would truly be fighting to rescue babies.

For me, motherhood looks a bit different than it looks for others. It does not consist of diaper changes, story time, and rocking with lullabies before sleep. Rather than holding my children in my arms, I hold them in my heart. I mother their legacies. But that does not make me any less of a mother simply because you cannot see them here. The forever impact they've made on my life and how they've changed me are proof enough that I'm a mother. Their mother.

This is my motherhood journey thus far…

In February 2009, I found myself alone in a bathroom, staring at the two blue lines that would forever change my life. I was nineteen, unmarried, and completely terrified to discover I was pregnant. Yes, I always knew I wanted to be a mother, but not yet. Not now. Not like this…

Though I had grown up in a Christian, pro-life home, I never imagined this would happen to me. After all, I had planned on remaining a virgin until marriage. Yet, somehow along the way, the world had seduced me.

Feelings of panic and fear immediately gripped my heart and that dreadful word captured my thoughts—abortion. Culture told me it was my choice to decide whether or not I was ready to be a mother.

My mind was consumed with thoughts of the shame and humiliation that would come with telling those I knew and loved that I was a pregnant and unwed teen. I didn't want people to discover the lifestyle I was leading. I didn't want to face the pain sure to come with choosing parenting or adoption. I didn't want my body to change from pregnancy. I didn't want permanent ties to the baby's father. I didn't want my entire future as I thought it should be to be forever altered. I could be a mother when I was ready, but it wasn't then. I convinced myself that having an abortion was my only option and the only solution.

Because I was only six weeks into gestation, and it was a pill I would be taking and not a surgical procedure, I convinced myself that it wasn't really an abortion. Because I couldn't feel any movement yet, never heard the fast thump, thump, thump of the baby's heart beating, and my belly was not yet round with child, I thought it wasn't a big deal. I could push thoughts of this new life within out of my mind and heart.

I wish I could tell you that I did not take that little pill that I thought would solve all my problems, but I did on February 6th, 2009, a day that will be etched into my memory forever. If only I had known that even though I was ending my pregnancy I would still feel that I would always be in some way, a mother.

Immediately after the abortion, relief washed over me, and I was ready to get back to my normal life and forget the nightmare ever happened. However, the pain quickly began catching up with me. I drowned my inexpressible sorrow in things like partying, drinking, and dating a new guy. I so desperately wanted to fill that empty, gaping wound in my heart.

Just a few short months later, I found myself once again sitting in a bathroom, alone with my thoughts, and another positive pregnancy test.

Yet again I had the same choice to make. How could this be my life? How had I gotten so far from what I had been taught and what I believed about abstinence, purity, and the sanctity of life? I was digging myself deeper and deeper into a pit of destruction and despair and I was too broken and weak to pull myself out. The agony and despair that I felt within the depths of my very soul were overwhelming and all encompassing.

I was sick of things as they were and felt ready to get my life together. I just needed to have this one last abortion and then I could move on. I reasoned that I had already had one abortion, so what's another? My life appeared to be a hopeless, helpless mess and it was too late for me to have the beautiful God-scripted story that I had longed for. Little did I know that my Heavenly Father was not surprised by my choices and He still had a plan...far beyond anything I could imagine or comprehend.

The appointment was set at Planned Parenthood for August 15th, 2009, just three days after my 20th birthday and a half a year after my first abortion. After August 15th, I would get my life together. After August 15th, I could move on and have a fresh start.

The day of my scheduled abortion came and went and my baby was still safely growing in my womb. This time around I could not bring myself to walk back into that office. God was fighting for me just as He was fighting for the life of the one who grew within me. He would not allow me to make the same mistake twice.

The Lord made it abundantly clear that I had come to a fork in the road and had a very big decision to make. He whispered to my heart that if I chose to have another abortion, I couldn't imagine the pain and darkness that would follow. But, if I chose *life*, I couldn't imagine the beauty that He would bring.

On a lovely August evening around dusk, I was alone with my thoughts, watching the pink clouds dance across the sky. It was in that moment that the decision suddenly became clear to me. I knew what I had to do. I had to obey Him…and choose life. Although I didn't know what would happen next or where He would lead me, having answers to my questions no longer mattered because He was with me. He promises to give us just what we need the moment we need it. There must have been rejoicing in Heaven on that summer evening in August when my child's life was saved.

The choice was no longer between abortion, adoption, and parenting, but now only between adoption and parenting, both of which ended with my child having life. For a time, I truly believed I was going to choose adoption. After wrestling with the decision for weeks, however, God showed me that His plan for me was parenting.

Early in my pregnancy, the Lord revealed to me that I was carrying a little girl named Lily, which means purity and innocence. Lily was to be a symbol of my renewed purity and redemption in Jesus Christ. I selected Katherine to be her middle name, not realizing at the time that Katherine also means purity. In Christ, I am washed white as snow.

My God was with me when I chose life for my daughter and through all the months I carried her, He sustained me. He was with me when I told my family the news that there would be someone joining the family. He was with them when He supplied the love and grace needed to accept me back home. He provided every penny needed when I didn't know how I would pay for doctor and hospital bills without insurance.

Seven months later, He was with me when I arrived at the hospital to deliver my daughter, two days past my due date, after a healthy and normal pregnancy. He was with me on that dark, stormy day, March 16th, 2010, when that little monitor was put up to my swollen belly and those dreadful words filled my ears, "I'm so sorry. Her heart is no longer beating." He was with me in the quiet, early-morning stillness, as I waited to deliver the body of my daughter who was already waiting for me in Heaven. He was with me when I held the body of my precious flower, Lily Katherine, who whispered goodbye before I had the chance to say hello. He was with me when the silence threatened to suffocate me.

He was with me through the loneliest night of my life as I cried from the very depths of my soul, lying in my hospital bed with the body of my lifeless daughter beside me. He was with me during those few precious, sacred moments I spent alone with her, giving her the hugs and kisses that would have to last a lifetime. He was with me the next afternoon as a blanket was placed over her tiny body and she was pushed down the hallway away from me, never to be held by her mommy again. He was with me when leaving the hospital with empty arms, a broken heart, and shattered dreams. Full of so many questions, He was with me when no answers could explain why she was taken so soon. He was with me as I watched her tiny casket, placed inside her cozy Moses basket, lowered into the opened Earth and showered with tears, rose and lily petals, and dirt.

Lily Katherine's name took on a whole new meaning. She will forever be pure and innocent. I struggled with wondering why God would let me carry Lily for all those months and love her so much, only to take her from me. But I have peace in knowing I made the choice to let God be God, to let God give and God take away. I can rest assured that I did the right thing by obeying Him. My daughter died with dignity.

How can I possibly capture in just a few paragraphs all that Lily's life means to me? God saved her from abortion and used her life to save mine. He used her to bring me back to Himself. He used her to bring healing from my abortion. He used her to restore family relationships and friendships.

I have given my first child the dignity of having a name, as an acknowledgement that he existed. I believe the Lord has revealed to me that my first baby was a boy. I've named him Luke Shiloh, meaning light and peace, because God has brought light in the midst of the deepest darkness and peace to my wounded, aching heart.

If you choose life, no matter the outcome, you'll have no regrets. These aren't empty words from someone who doesn't understand and has never walked this road. I can say "I get it" because I truly do. I've walked the road twice and I've chosen both ways, and I will forever regret my abortion, but I will never, ever regret choosing life. Even if I had known from the beginning that Lily would go home to Jesus before drawing her first breath. God has a wonderful, beautiful plan and purpose for each being created in His image.

My story is full of brokenness and heart-wrenching pain, yes, but please don't allow that to be what you take away from reading this. It is my hope and prayer that the lasting legacies of Luke and Lily will make an imprint on your heart. And that my story will point your eyes to redeeming, merciful Jesus, who brings beauty from ashes and makes whole what was once broken. He truly works all things together for our good and His glory.

The Lord used both my two babies who never spoke a word or took a single breath to forever change my life and future. For me, motherhood is keeping my promise to Lily and Luke to always be their voice, to share their lives and legacies, to speak out about the beauty and sanctity of each irreplaceable, individual life. I now write regularly on my blog and on other websites and speak all over the country, sharing my story of darkness to light. At one point I never wanted anyone to know about Lily and Luke, but now I want the world to know they are my children and I am their mother.

This is but a glimpse into my mother heart. To some, it may appear that I have no children. But, I can assure you, I do. They may not be alive on Earth, but they are more alive than you and I will ever be here, dancing eternally with Jesus on streets of gold. There is so much more to my bittersweet journey of motherhood and I believe there will be more pages the Lord will script in days to come. This is where He's brought me thus far. This is how He's given me a passion and a purpose to rescue precious babies. The dream I had as a little girl has come true.

"Motherhood was the great equalizer for me; I started to identify with everybody...as a mother, you have that impulse to wish that no child should ever be hurt, or abused, or go hungry, or not have opportunities in life."

— Annie Lennox, singer —

Courage Soup
Amber Coleman-Mortley

The glorious moments of my demise are numerous in relation to my dealings with my daughters. There is no extent to which they will not challenge my idea of how children should behave and what they are capable of. I take pride in the idea that I parent through logic and love. They keep me on my toes, keep my mind alert, and keep my parenting repertoire full.

On a normal evening my daughters take their bath together.

Often the baths will last twenty or thirty minutes, just because I need the time to keep them at bay so that I can ramp-up my love-o-meter into overdrive for the remaining forty-five minutes to an hour of the lights out routine.

This evening started out no different than any other evening. We were all ready for bed. We'd spent the entire day out of the house, part of which was at the circus. By the time I placed my lovernauts into the tub, I was completely done mentally, emotionally, and physically. I lay in the hall by the bathroom, spending their bath segment unwinding on mobile Twitter, Instagram, and Facebook.

The bath was winding down. My five-year-old decided she had to go to the bathroom, so she asked to get out of the tub. The four-year-old decided she needed to go as well, waited her turn, and then got out of the tub to take care of business. I decided that this unexpected five minute break should constitute another five minutes in the tub. Boy was I wrong. Against my better judgment, I left them in the tub and sat down on the floor in the doorway. I looked up at the ceiling, closed my eyes, and let out a heavy sigh. What a long day.

Suddenly I heard them scream.

My girls are precocious, dramatic, dynamic—normal kid qualities. They work hard at creating trouble for each other and ultimately for me. I love it only because I imagine all of the grief my siblings and I created for our mother. I see my reaction to their antics as my badge of honor, an earning of stripes or paying my dues. I commend their creativity and I love their variety. That is why when the screaming commenced I couldn't visualize any major atrocity that required an unraveling of my best parenting tactics and diplomacy.

In an instant, I was yanked back into reality by the horrendous commotion and shrill clamoring of my older two girls. My assumption was that someone took a nibble out of her sister in protest of sharing a toy. I honestly would have preferred that to what I saw. I stumbled into the bathroom to find the older two out of the tub, shivering, screaming, and pointing. The two-year-old stood in the tub saying, "No, no Mommy." *What could it be?* I thought to myself in horror. I carefully leaned over the edge and discovered that my youngest had relieved herself in the tub.

I wiped up all the kids, wrapped them in towels, and sent them to their room. How was I going to clean this? I stood there examining the situation like an engineer examines a river ripe for a bridge. I went through each possible scenario in my head.

I thought about catching it like a fish, or letting it just go down the drain. I thought of picking it up with a plastic fork. I was honestly stumped on this one. My germaphobic nature somehow created a bomb timer in my mind and therefore the anxiety rose with each passing second.

Just reach in there and let out the water, I said to myself. I couldn't. It was bubble bath soup. I let out another heavy sigh. How could she do this to me? *Okay, Amber, don't be a punk. Just reach in there and pull out the stopper.*

My other voice chimed in. *Wait! If you let out all of the water, you'll be left with an even bigger mess.*

The back and forth lasted for seconds, but it felt like hours. Finally, I just dove in. I was wasting time. I figured if I'd experienced projectile vomit in my face, birthed three kids naturally, experienced the fourth trimester, and cleaned up all kinds of whatever, I could do this and earn my mommy badge for this challenge.

As I began to execute my newly-administered job description of sanitation worker, I recalled all of the moments when my own mother sat by my bedside or carried me some place so that I could do x, y, or z after I left half of it someplace else. All the times that I watched her do the same for my siblings and realized that those moments were why we loved her so much.

I wasn't mad at my youngest daughter. She was almost completely potty trained at two. So I cleaned up the tub; I bleached *everything* and then finished the bedtime routine as per usual. For that night's prayer and thanksgiving meditation, I focused on how lucky I was to have daughters who do crazy things that push me to be stronger than I thought I was.

I Am a Capable Mom
Shawna Scafe

I am a capable mom.

If I say it enough times I will believe it.

Even more if I put myself in situations that are tricky, or overwhelming, or tiring then I cannot doubt it because success isn't always doing it flawlessly but rather simply doing it.

A buffalo-sized blind spot in my parenting was believing I was not capable.

I underestimated what I could take on as a mother and what my kids could endure or accomplish. I created an anxious atmosphere in the home where I would always say no to my husband. When he wanted some time away, to work overtime, or to run out for errands. If the kids weren't napping I would say no. I wouldn't cook certain things when I was alone with the kids because I had this notion that more dishes and complicated recipes had no privilege in my day. I was too tied up being a mom. I would opt to stay inside rather than bundle up and get the kids out of the house. Chasing a curious baby, constantly removing small objects from her mouth, playing with an unstoppable toddler sounded too tiring for a tired mom.

I was stranded on parent island with wild cavemen children. I wasn't capable of managing all of this.

It was unfair to my family. It was insecure of me.

Thankfully God has placed some wonderful moms in my life. These moms *do things* with their kids, *do things* for themselves and tote their kids along. They don't think, or justify, they just *do* and everyone finds a place to land and make it work. Even when it doesn't work their kids are still learning about being a little uncomfortable and adapting.

I've said it before, I am trying to do the opposite of my initial reactions, to stop imposing so many rules.

When plans are presented, spontaneous or not, I try and make my head nod no matter what is rising in my throat. My counters are lined with a layer of dishes, which still is a big mental block for me (ahem, recovering perfectionist) and I'm trying to fill every single day with something fun out of the house, or something new, or something messy for the kids.

When my husband asks to do something, now I tell him he doesn't need my permission but if he took a kid along that would be cool too. I know his heart gets tired too and he needs a break as much as I do. We try to each get an afternoon to ourselves on his days off, which has given me some guaranteed space to do whatever fills my heart. What do you do that fills your heart?

Do me a favor. Finish this sentence about you as a mother. Even if you don't fully believe it yet, state it aloud and own it. What is a struggle that has draped over your heart, been a block in your thinking, held you back? Discard it and finish this sentence.

I am a _____ mom!

Full Circle
Sheila Atkins
co-written by Jillian Amodio

I have two daughters. They are smart, beautiful, and so very loved. But for the longest time, I didn't even know if one of them was alive, or if she even knew I existed.

To understand my story you need to know a little bit about my childhood, although I suppose that's kind of where everyone's story starts.

I grew up a very spoiled child. I was the oldest and only girl out of six siblings. My parents gave us everything we ever wanted, well tangibly speaking. The only thing they failed to give us was love in its most basic form. I had everything I could have ever wanted. You'd think I would have been appreciative, but gratitude wasn't something I seemed capable of showing.

Looking back, all I ever wanted was to be loved, truly loved. I wanted words of affirmation. I needed to hear that my parents cared. Not to say that my parents were horrible people. They both grew up poor and tried to give us everything they never had. So I guess they loved us in the only way they knew how. They equated love with money, unfortunately, that's not what I needed.

By the time I was sixteen, I could not remember the last time my parents said I love you.

My parents were fairly strict with us, but strict doesn't mean much if naivety prevails.

I was a closet rebel. I partied behind my parents backs and they never were the wiser. I was young, I was stupid, and I found myself pregnant right after my sixteenth birthday. I was scared and I was confused, I tried to ignore it for a while. However, I had to accept the fact that I was pregnant when I started to feel the baby move inside of me.

I experienced an extreme range of emotions. I don't think I was really emotionally mature enough to understand what was happening and what needed to be done.

I never even told my parents I was pregnant. It got to be kind of obvious when I was about six months pregnant. Instead of asking me, they asked a friend of mine. She told them the truth. Really, they were the last ones to know. Just about everyone else around me knew I was pregnant; they didn't have a clue.

My mother yelled and my father ignored me. I was never really close to my mother but idolized my father, and I felt like I let him down. The first thing my mother said to me was "Is it too late to have an abortion?"

That was the whole reason I didn't tell them to begin with. I wanted to make my own decision. She (I always knew my baby was a she and never even had a sonogram to prove it) was my baby and I had to be the one to make the decisions.

When I was about three or four months pregnant, I had started to research my options. With four younger brothers (my fifth brother was born after I had my daughter) I considered asking my parents if I could keep her. I thought maybe my parents could help raise her. Ultimately I decided that I didn't want my mother raising my baby the way that she had raised me and my siblings. I wanted more for my baby. I wanted her to know love for what it truly was. I wanted her to form secure emotional attachments with her parents.

I considered abortion briefly but never really thought it an option because I had already formed an emotional attachment from the moment I knew she existed.

After finally discovering that I was pregnant, my pregnancy was never discussed again in our family. Physically I was pregnant, very pregnant! But we never talked about it.

My mother was brought up Catholic; my father was the son of a Baptist preacher. We were raised with no religion at all. I had no idea what I wanted in terms of religion for my daughter.

My mother decided that I should contact Catholic Charities. At eight months pregnant, I talked with a representative from the organization about the pros and cons of adoption.

I was still a little wild and naïve myself. Perhaps I was even a bit of a dreamer. I loved this baby. I connected with her. She was mine, and I kept trying to see if there was some way that I could settle down on my own. No matter how hard I tried, I could not imagine how I could possibly give my child any sort of life. I loved her, but that wasn't enough. She deserved more and I was determined to make sure she had it.

A month after I met with Catholic Charities, I went into labor. I never even called my parents. It was St. Patrick's Day and my friends were on their way over to hang out. They ended up taking me to the hospital instead.

She was the most beautiful baby in the world. I had her for two days, and those two days changed my life. I tried and tried to figure out a way that I could keep her. I just could not wrap my head around it.

I couldn't give her much, but I was determined to give her something. I gave her a name, Debra Karen. It was put on her birth certificate but somehow that copy never made it to the adoption agency.

The worst moment of my life was when my mother came to visit us in the hospital. She looked at her and held her for a minute. "I talked to your dad," she said, "and if you want to you can bring her home."

I knew my baby didn't deserve that. It was not a choice that I wanted to make. My parents never even asked me what I wanted, and now they simply decided to try to make the decision for me. Now that my mom and dad had agreed that I could keep her, it made it unbearable to walk out of the hospital without my baby.

A hole had been left in my heart. I felt empty.

Somehow life went on.

I had been home schooled for the last few months of my pregnancy because back then you were not allowed in school past a certain point; I guess they thought it set a bad example. Tutors were sent to my home each day. I went back to school the following year.

Six weeks after my daughter was born I drove back to Catholic Charities to sign the papers, finalizing the adoption process. I guess I never really considered where she would go once I left the hospital. I imagined she would be immediately placed with a family. It turns out she was transferred to a different hospital which would be listed as her place of birth. I found out later, on her thirty-fourth birthday, that she was alone for two months before she was finally adopted. That shattered my heart.

I believed that I was signing a piece of paper saying that if she should ever come looking for me, she could have my contact information. Sadly that's not what happened. I later found out that when she was in second grade, her mom mailed a letter with her picture in it to Catholic Charities and asked that they forward it to me. They mailed it back to her instead. On her eighteenth birthday, Samira (the beautiful name given to her by her adoptive parents), contacted Catholic Charities to request any information they had about me, her birth-mother. They said the file was closed but that she could pay $500 to reopen it and start a search. After some discussion, they decided not to reopen the file to avoid the heartache that would come should they find out I didn't want anything to do with her.

For thirty-four years I never stopped thinking about her. For thirty-four years I never stopped loving her. I would google her several times a year, and always on her birthday. I wanted to be sure she was okay. Was she happy? Was she safe? Was she even alive? I began to wonder.

I had always hoped she would come looking for me; I started to think that maybe she didn't want to know who I was. I never hired anyone to search for her because I felt like it was not my right to be that invasive. I truly thought that if she wanted to find me, it would be as easy as going to the adoption agency.

By that point I had my second daughter. She was born eleven years after Samira. On what would be Samira's thirty-fourth birthday, I happened to go by my mom's house. It was on St. Patrick's Day 2013. My mom and I were still not close, but we tried. I went over to have dinner with her.

When I came home that evening, I started thinking about Samira (who was still Debra to me). I googled her, and Samira was the first one that came up in the adoption search. I was shocked; I had been doing this very same thing for years and never found a match. This time was different, all of the facts matched. From the little she did find out from her adoption file it sounded like this Samira Perry (Perry was her married name) could actually be my daughter. I finally realized that she had been searching for me just as I had been searching for her. She did look for her file, she did try to find me, she just didn't have all the pieces.

I freaked out. My husband was sleeping beside me. I read about my daughter, my beautiful daughter. She was married and working on her master's degree. Oddly enough both she and my daughter Amanda had married men with the last name Perry. Two sisters who had never met ended up sharing the same last name.

I sent my daughter Amanda a text: *I think I just found your sister and she has the same last name as you!*

From the time that Amanda was four or five she always knew she had an older sister. She was the one who actually sent Samira an email first. Samira lived in Arizona. The day after her birthday she woke up to emails from us.

The only reason Samira even opened the email was because it was from someone with the same last name as her husband. She figured it was from a family member of his.

I got a text from Amanda while I was at work: *she emailed me back.*

I spent the entire work day emailing between Amanda and Samira trying to figure out if we were all really family! As soon as Samira received the email, she called her husband at work. He left immediately and came home to be with her. When I found that out, I knew he was one great guy.

The next day, once our emotions were a little more under control, I ended up talking to her on the phone for over an hour! I could not believe that I was speaking to my firstborn child. My heart felt whole again.

Samira informed us that from the little information she was able to get from her file, she knew that my family owned a trucking company. At one point, she even went to a local library and got a phonebook for Maryland. Her mom helped research and they started to write down the names of each company listed. She told me later that she had initially planned to call each one and just start asking questions, but she couldn't think of what to say or what to ask so she just kept staring at the list and never made the call.

We both had a lot of what ifs. But it didn't matter anymore. We had found each other.

A couple of days later she asked if her mom could talk to me. It was hilarious; for thirty-four years her mother had worried that she was letting me down! Her adoptive father was Catholic but quit practicing, her mother was Jewish. Samira was raised Jewish, and her mother worried that she was letting me down because I had handed her over to Catholic Charities. She told me that she always wanted Samira to know her birth-mother.

Everything I heard was great. She had a wonderful childhood. The kind of life she deserved to grow up living. The kind of life I couldn't give her. Everything I worried about was for nothing, she was happy, she had a sister who was also adopted, they traveled, and they were loved. Her life was what I had dreamed of for her.

Knowing all of this took the biggest weight off of my shoulders. The weight I had carried since I was sixteen years old. Everyone says that my entire attitude has changed since I found my daughter.

As crazy as it sounds, the first twelve to fourteen years of her life, she lived less than an hour away from me.

It was unbelievable.

May 8, the week of Mother's Day, was the first day I got to see her since I had held her in the hospital. My husband and I went to the airport to pick her and her husband up. I could see them coming up the terminal and it seemed like the longest hallway. I was restraining myself from running through security to see her. We held onto each other and cried. The man at the airport said, "It's too emotional for me around here; you guys are making me cry."

It was like coming home. I didn't want to let her go.

At the time, my father was very sick. She was a hospice social worker and she got to meet my dad, her grandfather. When she went back home she talked with people she worked with and got him medical equipment to make his last few months more bearable. Everything fit together so beautifully. The last grandchild he got to meet was actually his first. He loved her immediately, all of us did. She even came back for his funeral in July.

We live hours apart in completely different parts of the country. But we are as close as we could be! We talk regularly. She knows her sister, her nieces, her aunts, uncles, cousins, her entire other family. Overnight she went from having a very small family to one that was larger than life!

I now have a tattoo of both of my girl's names as a constant reminder of the love that I have for them. I always wanted a tattoo but could never come up with something that I loved enough to have on my body forever. Two days before Samira came to visit for the first time, I got a tattoo that I am in love with. Both of the girl's names are intertwined with flowers that are the color of their birthstones.

It is crazy to think that it took thirty-four years, but everything has finally come full circle.

"For I know the plans I have for you, declares the Lord, plans for welfare and not for evil, to give you a future and a hope."

— Jeremiah 29:11 —

Contributing Authors

Hannah Rose Allen

Through her own experience with unplanned pregnancy, abortion, and the loss of a child, Hannah Rose has become dedicated to ministering the love of Jesus to others as a writer and speaker. Website: www.roseandherlily.com

Jillian Amodio

Jillian is an author, writer, wife, and mother. There is no job she finds more rewarding than being a mom. She loves yoga, coffee, God, and her family! Website: www.jillianamodio.com

Sheila Atkins

Shirley Bailey

Mom to three beautiful children. Life is hard, but we can make it beautiful.

Kaytlin Brown

Celi Camacho

Author/Illustrator of *Bedtime for Meaghan*, wife and crafty mother of two great kids. Lover of drawing and creating beauty. Website: www.time2refuel.wordpress.com

Gail Centeno

Wife, mom, photographer, blogger. Ridiculously busy, completely imperfect, saved by grace, coffee lover. Website: www.gailcentenophotography.com

Carin Clark

Carin is a mother of three, writer, blogger and entrepreneur who lives in the Washington, DC metro area. She is the owner and author of the parenting and family site Memoirs of a Clueless Woman. Website: www.clueconsultingllc.net/blog-mrscpkc

Amber Coleman-Mortley

Haiku Bio:

Amber is a mom

Who runs a blog and a vlog

Parenting is love

Website: www.MomOfAllCapes.com

Lori Cooper

Jennifer Daiker

I'm a children's book writer, a photo enthusiast, and the mother of a beautiful baby girl. Website: www.jenscraplandia.wordpress.com

Kristi Dalnoky

I'm Kristi—wife/mommy, author of *Klover House*, and aspiring entrepreneur. I spend my days enjoying my three, precious daughters, putting my cooking skills to the test, and growing as a child of God. Website: www.kloverhouse.blogspot.com

Tammy Darrow

Jessica Dugan

Beck Gambill

I became a mama on accident, but I'm finding that God gives good gifts, even one's we didn't know we wanted. I'm an uncalled mama, leaning heavily on Jesus. I'm looking for mercy at every turn. Website: www.beckgambill.wordpress.com

Hillary Gould

I have been married for twelve years and have three children. My first two children are thirteen months apart, and my second two are twenty months apart. I stay at home and am home schooling my sweet gifts from God.

Deanna Herrmann

I'm currently a stay-at-home mom, an expat living in Germany, and author of *From Casinos To Castles*. I spend my time with my two loves, my husband and son. Website: www.fromcasinostocastles.com

Raquel Kato

CarmenAna Klosterman

Mother of seven, home schooler of my children for eighteen years. I am now a proud mother and grandmother of three beautiful children.

Michelle Love

Thomasina Martin

I'm the single mother to a wonderful little boy. Our lives are hectic and filled with the busyness that life brings. With love and prayer we manage to survive.

Stephanie Messa

I'm a mom/wife/blogger/laugh-maker/all around sassy lady in a black dress—aka, black yoga pants. Website: www.themominblack.com

Rachael Moshman

Rachael Moshman, M.Ed. is a mom, freelance writer, and blogger. She is passionate about adoption, pizza, and the color pink. Website: www.rachaelmoshman.com

Amy Orzechowski

Stephanie Page

Stephanie is a wife and mom to three girls. Her heart is to see people living their lives on purpose for the glory of God. She spends her time as a speaker, writer, bible study leader, and conference planner. Website: www.stephaniempage.com

Amanda Perry

I am a wife to a wonderful man and a mother to three beautiful girls. I am enjoying every minute of it!

Donna Reedy

I am a mom to four human children and many more four-legged ones. I have done home daycare for over twenty years. My children are my life, and I truly believe that every child is precious.

Carla Rogers

I love finding ways to serve God within my day to day activities. I am also getting good at taking a leap of faith. I am a wife and hopefully at some point a mother to an adopted child.

L. Rodgers

Shawna Scafe

Married SAHM to two toddlers in small town Canada. Sharing my honest mom fails, hard truths about marriage, weird things I've been googling, random DIYs, family food, and other nerdy things. Website: http://www.dovetailblog.com/

Anna Schatzman

Dr. Barbara Sorrels

Dr. Barbara Sorrels's own experience as a parent, teacher, caregiver, university professor, consultant, and children's pastor brings a relatable quality to her work, speaking, and writing. She is Executive Director of The Institute for Childhood Education, a professional development firm for those who live and work with children. Website: www.DrBarbaraSorrels.com

Amy Stoddard

I am a stay-at-home mommy to my four beautiful children. I believe that God never gives us more than we can handle.

Lee U.

Ann Van De Water

I am a mom of three sons and author of a humorous book about motherhood entitled *Mommy Memoirs*—a collection of candid and real-life tales about raising our boys. I am passionate about motherhood! Connect with me by signing up for my newsletter. Website: www.annvandewater.com/blog/

Jessica Ward

Rebekah Wishart

Bonus Material

Five Things Everyone Should Know About Adoption
Patricia Jaber, MSW

Caring Adoptions
PJaber@CaringAdoptions.org
www.CaringAdoptions.org

1. Adoption Involves Trauma.

By definition, the relationship between parent and child – source and offspring, origin and progeny – must be terminated before an adoption can occur. No matter the specifics or context, adoption does not take place without the severance of a natural, biologically-affirmed connection. Such discontinuity, no matter how short lived, can cause trauma in the lives of those involved. Additionally, many adoptive parents endure harrowing circumstances in the course of their adoption journeys, often preceded by the trauma of infertility. Because trauma is inherent to any adoption process, it is natural and normal for those involved to feel some kind of pain or negative emotion about it, and those negative emotions are as important to address as those that are positive.

2. Honesty is Vital.

Honesty is a vital component of a healthy understanding of adoption or participation in an adoption journey. Adoption should NOT be considered a dirty secret; it is a loving, and purposeful choice. Commitment to an adoption plan for a child connotes sacrifice, vulnerability, and significant effort from both birth parents and adoptive parents; and honesty (throughout the process and the life of the adoptee) supports the healthiest outcomes for everyone involved.

3. Your Body is Your Business.

Much to the dismay of just about everyone, you do NOT have to talk about your reproductive choices if you don't want to – especially if they involve adoption! How any person comes to be involved with adoption – as a birthparent, an adoptive parent, or an adoptee – is his or her personal story, and deserves the same respect automatically given to biologically-formed families. Natural curiosity can cause intrusive interrogations, but there are many ways to understand, educate, and advocate adoption without sharing personal stories or violating confidentiality. Often unconsidered (but no less important) is the perspective of an adoptee and their right to know their story of origin before it is shared with everyone else.

4. Birthmothers Love Their Children.

Even if you cannot fathom any circumstance in which your parental rights would be terminated (voluntarily or involuntarily), please know that women who give birth are biologically motivated to love their children, regardless of how their love is demonstrated or perceived. All women (birthmothers included) express their emotions differently and could show their love in ways that might seem foreign or even inappropriate to you, but this does not make their love any less real to them. A birthmother's voluntary relinquishment of her child into an adoption plan is the most selfless, caring, and loving option when she cannot care for her child herself. Birthmothers do NOT give anything away when their children are adopted; instead, they share the love of their child with another family.

5. The Love in Adoption is Miraculous, and Can Change Our World.

Adoption is all about love. Adoptees are persons who were too loved to remain in their biological family (for fear of or the actualized incapacity to provide for their welfare) and, therefore, were assumed into the love of an adoptive family. Adoptive parents engage in an exhausting adoption process so that they may share their love. If adoption planning was as widely accepted as a choice after pregnancy as is the (far too common) choice for unready persons to attempt to parent, fewer children would become involved in social systems of child protection, poverty, and cyclical violence. If those who become pregnant truly embrace their child's very best interest over their own selfish expectations, and ultimately identify themselves as unprepared for the life-changing responsibilities of parenthood, they can plan a life full of love for that child through adoption.

Patricia Jaber, MSW

Ms. Jaber graduated from Trinity University in San Antonio, Texas with a Bachelor of Arts in Sociology in 2007, and went on to work as a Child Protective Services Specialist III in their Family Preservation Program through 2010. After moving back home, Ms. Jaber assumed her current title as Post Placement Coordinator for Caring Adoptions of Houston, Texas in 2011. She graduated with her Masters of Social Work with honors from the University of Houston's Graduate College of Social Work in 2014.

Perinatal Mood and Anxiety Disorders

Birdie Gunyon Meyer, RN, MA

Postpartum Support International (PSI)

www.postpartum.net

1-800-944-4PPD (4773)

Perinatal Mood and Anxiety Disorders (PMAD) is a broad term that includes a set of disorders that can occur anytime during pregnancy and the first year after giving birth. This set of disorders includes depression, anxiety, panic, obsessive-compulsive disorder (including intrusive thoughts), post-traumatic stress disorder, bipolar disorder, and psychosis. A PMAD is the most common complication of pregnancy and childbirth. The term used by most people for this disorder is "Postpartum Depression".

Psychosis affects 1-2 women per one thousand births. Depression and anxiety occur more frequently, affecting 1 in 7 women. Many women and their families don't always recognize a PMAD.

What are some of the signs and symptoms of a PMAD that can occur?

Frequent crying, sleep and appetite changes, feelings of loneliness, sadness, or hopelessness, frequent mood swings, repetitive, sometimes scary thoughts that won't go away, anger, frustration, irritability, difficulty bonding with the baby, anxiety, panic, excessive worry, lack of interest in activities you used to enjoy, fatigue, feeling overwhelmed, feeling speeded up, or thoughts of harming yourself.

The Baby Blues affects 80% of new moms so it is important to know that you are not alone. This is a reaction to your changing hormones and adjusting to life with a new baby. The Baby Blues however, don't last longer than 2 weeks. If you are experiencing any of the signs and symptoms above beyond 2 weeks postpartum, it's not just the blues anymore.

Who develops a PMAD? What are the risk factors?

Those at higher risk for developing a mood or anxiety disorder during pregnancy or postpartum include—

A personal or family history of pregnancy or postpartum mood disorder, depression, anxiety, panic, obsessive-compulsive disorder (OCD), PTSD, bipolar disorder, or psychosis.

- History of severe PMS
- Thyroid disease or other endocrine disorders
- Lack of support from family and friends
- A history of sexual, physical, verbal, or mental abuse
- Pregnancy complications and/or a traumatic birth
- Chronic sleep deprivation
- History of previous pregnancy losses
- Major life stressors
- Health Issues with mom or baby

How do I get better?

The good news is you can get better. Educate yourself and your loved ones. Eat a balanced diet and keep moving. Go for walks, get sleep when you can, and don't hesitate to ask for help. Remember to take time for yourself, to refresh, refill, and relax.

Where do I find more information about Perinatal Mood and Anxiety Disorders? Where can I find help?

Postpartum Support International (PSI) www.postpartum.net offers support from volunteers around the U.S. and 40 countries around the world. You will also find helpful information and the volunteer coordinators will connect you with local resources in your community.

PSI has a Warmline in both English and Spanish. 1-800-944-4PPD (4773) There is also a weekly Chat with an Expert. http://postpartum.net/Get-Help/PSI-Chat-with-an-Expert.aspx

Other helpful websites:

www.postpartumprogress.com

www.ppdsupportpage.com

www.postpartumstress.com

www.postpartumdads.org

Remember
You are not alone. You are not to blame. With treatment, you will get better.

Birdie is an RN with a Master's in Counseling. She is a Past-President of Postpartum Support International (PSI) and is currently serving as the Chair of Education and Training. Birdie is a PSI PMAD International Trainer and speaks frequently to communities, nursing schools, grand rounds, and conferences. Birdie specializes in the recognition and treatment of pregnancy and postpartum mood and anxiety disorders. She is the coordinator of the Perinatal Mood Disorders Program at Indiana University Health in Indianapolis, IN. Birdie is highlighted as a PMD expert in PSI's DVD that is shown around the country. "Healthy Mom, Happy Family: Understanding Pregnancy and Postpartum Mood and Anxiety Disorders".

bmeyer@postpartum.net or bmeyer2@iuhealth.org
317-363-4622 or 317-962-8191

Stand Up Girl Foundation
Executive Director, Dawn Marie Perez

StandUpGirl.com

DearBecky@standupgirl.com

About: The StandUpGirl Foundation is a 501(c)3 charitable organization dedicated to providing pregnant adolescent and young adult women with alternatives to abortion. The mission is to change hearts and save lives by educating young women on the development of the unborn child and alternatives to abortion.

1. What advice do you have for young women who may feel afraid and alone when facing an unplanned pregnancy?

There are organizations in your neighborhood that are there for you. You are never really alone. The women at these local centers have been in the same situation you have and will be there to help you every step of the way, no matter what decision you choose for you and your baby. They will be your friend, support system and family!

2. What is one of the most inspiring stories you have heard in your line of work?

We receive so many inspiring stories from women every day who have chosen life for their unborn children. Any young woman who decides to give life to her baby, especially when she is feeling alone, unloved and ill-equipped, is a heroine in my eyes.

3. Do you agree that no matter who you are, all mother's to be at some point feel overwhelmed and anxious?

Every mother goes through feelings of doubt. That is totally normal. It doesn't matter if you are young, old, single, or married. You are venturing into something new, a new path for your life and there will always be feelings of doubt. But, you are equipped with just what you need...love! A loving, caring, forgiving, and guiding mother is more important than any amount of money, big house, or fancy car...babies and children need LOVE!

4. Where can women, especially teenagers, go for support and financial assistance when facing an unplanned pregnancy?

Anyone who finds themselves in an unplanned pregnancy should go to www.StandUpGirl.com or to www.OptionLine.com. Both of these organizations will get you in contact with a local pregnancy center in your neighborhood that can help you with food, clothing, childcare, job hunting, and financial services like WIC (Women Infants and Children). Don't ever let someone convince you that your financial status is not what it should be to raise a child. There are an abundance of resources to help you, and they are free for those who need them.

5. Even though it can seem that way, is an unplanned pregnancy really the end of the world?

Never is an unplanned pregnancy the end of the world. It is the beginning of a new chapter in your life. The chapter might be out of order from what you had originally planned your life story to be like, but all of your goals and aspirations can still be met with a child. In fact, those goals will now be so much grander once completed!

6. Do you offer support forums or ways for moms-to-be to interact and see that they are not alone in their situations?

StandUpGirl.com is a living, breathing website that is active 24/7 with young women interacting with each other through our forums, blogs, chat rooms, and text counseling services. Our volunteers come from around the world, so we can communicate with girls from different regions. Twelve separate forums exist: "Personal Experiences", "Pregnancy Questions", "Parent Talk", "Complications During Pregnancy", "I think I'm Pregnant, Now What?", "After the Choice", "Need Advice", "A Guy Says", and "Parent Talk for Dads", as well as site feedback forums. The forums are very active, and posts are added several times a day. Visitors also send emails to the StandUpGirl's, who respond to them daily. This provides visitors to the site with the knowledge, clarity, empowerment, and self-confidence needed to make decisions for their life in "real-time.

7. Do you have any advice for young moms-to-be when it comes to telling friends and family about their pregnancies?

We recommend that honesty is always the best policy. Your family and friends might at first be in shock, but they will calm down and things will settle once they see how strong and confident you are with regards to your child and your future. In time they will come along side you and support you. Most grandparents melt the moment they see that cute little bundle of joy! If things do not turn out how you expected or hoped for, rest assured knowing that we are here to stand alongside you and support you no matter what. We will also help you to find the resources in your neighborhood so you have someone local to be your support and "family".

8. It is certainly true that motherhood can be difficult, but is there anything more rewarding?

Being the mother of a 2 year old and our second child on the way, I can't think of anything in my life that has been as rewarding as having and raising my daughter. The joy and love she brings to my life can't be described in words. Her unconditional love cannot be measured in any form.

Resources: StandUpGirl.com is a rapidly growing website whose scope is world-wide. We have "StandUpGirls" – volunteers who moderate the site's chat rooms and forums and respond to emails from across the United States as well as in Canada, South Africa and Japan. Young women from England, Australia, Canada, Russia, Africa, and South America – all over the world – are coming to StandUpGirl.com looking for information about pregnancy. They find educational material, real answers to their questions, and a community of women they can talk to about their unplanned pregnancy. The scope of StandUpGirl.com is only limited by the funds available to advertise it. Since our inception in 2000, we have had over 26 million visitors to our site and we are currently seeing over 400,000 per month along with another 295,000 visits per month to our Facebook page.

Ultimate Goal: To get the users in touch with local Pregnancy Resource Centers that can provide them with the personal interaction they need and a local support team. We currently refer our girls to www.OptionLine.org which offers 24/7 support along with an extensive worldwide contact list of Life Affirming Pregnancy Centers. Our recent endeavor with OptionLine has opened up a new resource for girls requesting help. In 2013, we added the option for young women to text PREGNANT to 313131 and they now have available 24 hour counseling support. During our first three weeks of trials, we had 45 girls come through StandUpGirl and text the support line. We are currently seeing almost 400 text conversations a month through this media. As technology changes and as our users get more mobile, we will have to develop more innovative ways to stay where users can easily attain access to our resources. We currently have an Android and iPhone App on the market for users to download which provides them access to our forums, videos, pregnancy symptoms, and support lines, including OptionLine.

6 things to remember when facing an unplanned pregnancy:

1. You are NOT alone. There are unlimited resources and organizations ready and willing to walk alongside you in your journey.

2. No pregnancy is really unplanned. We all have a purpose and there is a plan for each of us in this world.

3. You are brave and can do this! Becoming a mother will be one of the most joyous and rewarding experiences of your life and no one has the right to convince you otherwise.

4. YOU are the one who decides what is best for YOU and for your BABY. This is no one else's decision to make or to live with. Only yours!

5. Your goals and plans for your life have not ended. This is just the beginning of a new path to accomplishing those goals.

6. Never say "I can't." You will find a way to provide everything your child needs, but most of all, you will love them unconditionally!

Special Beginnings Birth & Women's Center
Ann Sober, RN, BSN

www.SpecialBeginnings.com

1454 Baltimore-Annapolis Blvd.

Arnold, MD 21012

410-626-8982

About: Special Beginnings is a licensed, CABC accredited, free-standing birth center located in Arnold, Maryland. The birthing center is staffed by experienced certified nurse-midwives (CNMs). They are proud to offer comprehensive health and wellness care for women.

1. What makes birthing centers like yours so unique?

We are all about offering women choices. Women have the choice of having their baby at the hospital with a midwife or at the actual birthing center, whereas oftentimes a pregnant mother feels like her only option is a typical hospital birth. In the state of Maryland for instance, it is rather difficult to find an opportunity to do a home-birth. Basically what we offer is to bring clients to our "home" and give them the personal birthing experience they desire. We do have a fixed emergency situation being central to the hospital should the need for emergency care arise.

2. What services does a midwife offer that traditional OBGYN's do not?

The service that we offer is the educational piece as well as the lifestyle piece because we are looking at the woman as a whole person rather than just as a pregnant uterus. We are looking at her lifestyle, her nutrition, her job…. We are looking at how her job impacts her craniosacral being and how that can impact her labor and delivery. Because we are not looking at pregnancy as an accident waiting to happen but rather something that is normal, things that are abnormal stand out to us right away. We are not going to take care of people who are outside of the scope of our practice. We are however part of the healthcare system so we do have the immediate access to refer a woman to someone who can care for her properly.

3. Who should consider a midwife?

Anyone can consider a midwife, we don't just provide services for women who are pregnant. We provide services to women throughout their life-cycle. Certified nurse midwives, like those we employ here are educated to care for a woman's reproductive health throughout their life. We begin caring for women from the time they first begin their menstrual cycles, to the time they become geriatric. We do provide things like annual physical exams. Basically women who are reasonably healthy and who don't have any sort of major health issues would do just fine with a midwife.

4. How can having a midwife alter or enhance a woman's pregnancy and birthing experience?

We have the time, and we take the time to have quality face to face interaction with each woman that we serve. We keep our clients very informed throughout every step and guide them to make their own decisions. Decisions are not ours to make, they are the clients. Sometimes of course we do not agree with the clients decisions, but we do respect them as best we can. We strive to be more personal and more client oriented.

5. Does the support of a midwife end once the baby is born?

Absolutely not! The care of a midwife continues for six more weeks and can of course continue with more routine gynecological and reproductive care.

6. Do you have any advice for women struggling with infertility?

Don't wait too long to seek out help and support.

7. What would you say to a new mother-to-be experiencing anxiety over the birthing experience?

Educate yourself. The more that you know, the less scary it will be. It's what you don't know that scares you. There are plenty of classes you can take and resources to go to, there are even people who will come to your house and teach birthing classes and relaxation techniques in your own home.

8. Do you have any advice for first time moms?

Investigate your options. Don't think that you have to do what everyone else is doing. Do your research and again educate yourself. Tour different facilities and see all of the options that are available to you to find out what best suits your needs. The other piece of advice I have is to not be afraid to leave a provider or practice and seek out someone else should you not feel comfortable or feel like your needs are not being met.

9. What advice or words of encouragement do you have for mothers wanting to experience an all natural or more natural birthing experience after having a hospital birth or cesarean section in the past?

You can do it! If you choose an option like a birthing center or a home-birth you are not locked in. Sometimes women are fearful to try something different because they fear that if they can't tolerate the pain or decide at any time to change their mind, they are stuck. This is not the case, you can always go to the hospital. Birthing centers like ours have hospital privileges and can provide you with access to everything the hospital has. If you have had a C-section in the past, you can attempt a vaginal birth, oftentimes it just has to be done in a hospital setting under the care of a midwife. Just because you have had a past cesarean birth does not necessarily mean you will have to have another.

10. It seems like a great deal of breastfeeding moms at some point face struggle, hardships, or concerns but don't know how to ask for help. What should all moms know about breastfeeding and where can they go for support?

There is a lot of support especially on-line. There is La Leche League and most hospitals have lactation consultants. We have a breastfeeding boutique and lactation consultants available. The whole thing is to recognize that although breastfeeding is normal, just as childbirth is normal, it can require a lot of support. People are there to help and assist you with whatever your individual needs may be.

11. If a family wishes to include an older sibling in the birth of a younger sibling what are some tips for going about this?

It is certainly an available option. Here at Special Beginnings children are welcome we just require that the child has a designated babysitter to tend to them at all times. Children are often interested in the birth of a new sibling, but not the duration and length of labor. They need to have the freedom to go somewhere else even if it is just to another room to watch television or play. If a child becomes alarmed at any point, all that is needed is an explanation of what is going on. It is not traumatizing if they are talked to and have someone there for them. It can be a very rewarding experience for the whole family.

12. Is the birth of a new life an amazing thing to witness or what?

I have been doing this for 47 years and it is always a miracle. I just can't tell you the power that it is to see this new person emerge into the world, turn and look at their mommy and nuzzle into her. It is just not explainable.

Additional Information:

Certified nurse-midwives are registered nurses who have completed an advanced educational program in midwifery accredited by the American College of Nurse Midwives (ACNM).

For more information about midwifery visit www.midwife.org

For more information about breastfeeding support visit La Leche League at www.llli.org

Check your local hospitals and birthing centers for prenatal and postnatal classes available to you.

Did you find this book helpful or inspirational?

Tell us about it.

Info@Causepub.com

Manufactured by Amazon.ca
Acheson, AB